Volume XIV, Number 8

Significant Issues Series

Investing in Security
Economic Aid for Noneconomic Purposes

HC
60
.B885
1992
West

by Stanton H. Burnett

foreword by Ernest Graves

The Center for Strategic
and International Studies
Washington, D.C.

Library of Congress Cataloging-in-Publication Data

Burnett, Stanton H.
    Investing in security : economic aid for noneconomic purposes /
by Stanton H. Burnett ; foreword by Ernest Graves.
        p. cm. — (Significant issues series, ISSN 0736-7136 ;
v. 14, no. 8)
    Includes bibliographical references.
    ISBN 0-89206-186-3
    1. Economic assistance, American—Developing countries—Case
studies. 2. United States—National security. 3. Developing
countries—Economic policy—Case studies. 4. Developing countries—
Social policy—Case studies. I. Title. II. Series.
HC60.B885 1992
338.9'17301724—dc20
                                      92-13676
                                         CIP

Contents

About the Author

Stanton H. Burnett is a senior adviser to CSIS and former director of studies. He joined CSIS in 1988 following his retirement as counselor of the United States Information Agency (USIA)—the senior professional position at the agency. Dr. Burnett worked for NBC and taught political science at Hobart and William Smith Colleges before going overseas with USIA. Among other foreign service assignments, he was counselor for public affairs in Rome and at the U.S. Mission to NATO in Brussels. In Washington, he has served as USIA's director of European affairs and director of research. While at CSIS, Dr. Burnett served as project director for the study producing this report.

Foreword

The cold war is over. The Western allies won. Doctrinaire communism, with its commitment to centrally planned economies, authoritarian government, and ultimate world hegemony, is thoroughly discredited and rejected wherever there is real freedom of choice.

The United States, however, still has a vital stake in the rest of the world. Poverty and disease, the narcotics trade, ethnic strife and the abuse of human rights, mass migration to escape oppressive conditions, nuclear proliferation and the spread of other weapons of mass destruction, local scarcity of natural resources, and environmental degradation all threaten regional stability. Together they constitute a serious drain on the vitality of the international system on which the United States depends. Unless abated, current trends could be catastrophic over the longer term.

During the cold war the United States employed security and economic assistance as major policy instruments in its rivalry with the Soviet Union. In combination they made a major contribution to the success of the Western alliance.

In many cases economic assistance was employed in the pursuit of noneconomic objectives, such as national security, democratization, and international stability. This strategy was and remains a controversial concept. Yet, almost inevitably, there will be occasions in the future when the leadership will fall back on methods used in the past.

How well did it work? What lessons can we learn from past experience with this strategy? To what extent would it be wise to employ economic aid in this way in the future? Given the economic problems that we face at home and abroad, we need answers to these questions to help guide the future use of aid in support of U.S. foreign policy.

Fortunately, the Pew Charitable Trusts took a particular interest in this subject and granted CSIS the support to carry out a two-year study of the problem. The Center undertook case studies of four strategically important countries where the United States has employed economic assistance for noneconomic purposes—South Korea, the Philippines, Pakistan, and Mexico. The study team also drew upon the results of other ongoing research at CSIS, including a study of the politics of economic reform in sub-Saharan Africa sponsored by the U.S. Agency for International Development.

In this final report Stanton H. Burnett has distilled the historical narratives, analyses, and insights of the case studies into a coherent, compelling set of findings on the use of economic aid as a policy instrument. For those concerned with the future employment of economic aid this study provides many valuable lessons.

Ernest Graves
Senior Adviser, CSIS
September 1992

Acknowledgments

It required an uncommon combination of participants to bring to its conclusion a study of issues of this size, complexity, and sensitivity. That fortunate combination contained three main elements.

First, the Pew Charitable Trusts played an intellectual role in the project that went beyond the funding that made it all possible. The conception of the study and all the shaping in the early stages had the full participation of that institution's officials, themselves scholars. It is too bad that they will remain anonymous to the citizens/taxpayers who stand to benefit from more enlightened decision making and investing in U.S. foreign policy.

As its partner in this work, Pew chose a research institution with particular strengths that were pointedly apt for carrying it out.

At the top of the list of those who left their intellectual mark on the study are Dr. Penelope Hartland-Thunberg and General Ernest Graves.

Dr. Thunberg, senior associate in International Business and Economics at CSIS, brought to the work government experience (as a staff economist with the Council of Economic Advisers and vice chairman of the Advisory Committee on East-West Trade, among others) and fine scholarship (her latest book: *China, Hong Kong, Taiwan and the World Trading System*). She started our process with a review of essential existing literature that became a wise guiding essay. Dr. Thunberg also contributed important sections of the background for the final report, as noted within, and was part of the lively debate on the implications of the findings.

General Graves is a senior adviser at CSIS whose expertise encompasses both foreign assistance and exactly those political and security issues at the heart of the study. Directly relevant to the work at hand, General Graves was director of Civil Works and deputy chief of the Army Corps of Engineers, director of the Defense Security Assistance Agency, and deputy secretary of defense for Security Assistance. He joined

CSIS's director of Asian Studies, Dr. Gerrit Gong, in supervising the four case studies, but then went on to provide the most cogent analyses of their implications.

Masterful coordination, from beginning to end, was provided by Dr. David Wendt. As director of Program Planning in the Office of Director of Studies at CSIS, Dr. Wendt had the task of weaving threads from all parts of the Center into this hypersynergistic effort.

The four case studies could not have been in better hands.

Ambassador Ernest H. Preeg, holder of the William M. Scholl Chair in International Business at CSIS, knows the Washington-Manila aid connection from both ends. He was chief economist at the U.S. Agency for International Development from 1986 to 1988, immediately following service as senior economic adviser for the Philippines. His case study has already become a book, *Neither Fish Nor Fowl: U.S. Economic Aid to the Philippines for Noneconomic Objectives,* that is playing an important role in Washington debates on aid.

Dr. Shireen T. Hunter is the author of *OPEC and the Third World: The Politics of Aid* and as deputy director of Middle East Studies watches Pakistan for CSIS. Her latest book is *Iran and the World: Continuity in a Revolutionary Decade.*

Dr. M. Delal Baer, deputy director of the Americas Program, is probably Washington's most frequently consulted— from hearings to media interviews—expert on Mexico and directs CSIS's Mexico Project. Her essay on North American free trade appeared in *Foreign Affairs* in 1991.

Dr. Michael J. Mazarr, senior fellow in International Security Studies, is an expert on Asian-Pacific security, at the heart of the Korea case study, and published *Missile Defenses and Asian-Pacific Security* in 1989. Dr. Mazarr's research on the ground in Korea was backed by Dr. William J. Taylor, vice president of CSIS and leader of the Center's International Security team, himself an expert on the two Koreas.

But perhaps the real heroes of this effort were an extraordinary group of congressional staffers and administration officials who labored through long meetings to give the project its original shape and then provided a wise (and severe) sounding board for the case studies and implications. Each of these dedicated men and women were adding these burdens to their regular schedules, driven only by their own devotion to sound U.S. policy.

Part One
Conclusions and Recommendations

Starting at the End: What the Study Means for Policymakers

Although the analyses done for this study have sparked controversies of interpretation among the groups steering the work (composed principally of social scientists from CSIS, congressional staffers expert in U.S. foreign assistance, and government officials bearing program responsibility), some findings are so clear and agreed that they constitute lessons of history that the future cannot responsibly ignore.

The overall record of U.S. economic assistance during the cold war period, of which this study analyzes a slice, is clearly a record studded with successes; the difficulties examined here do not detract from the fact that both globally and in many single countries the many programs that transferred U.S. resources to other nations in order to achieve U.S. foreign policy objectives did just that. Sometimes the paths taken were surprising; some of the successes were almost accidental, others were buried under failures, problems, and unintended consequences; some desired outcomes even came about *in spite of* conceptual failures on Washington's part. But U.S. economic and military assistance played a key role in winning the cold war and therefore *deserve* unblinking analysis in order to increase the odds for success in the new era.

The evidence provided by four full-scale country case studies was broadened by comparison with a CSIS study of similar issues in five sub-Saharan African countries and then by an informal search by the Center's regional study programs for significant cases that would contradict or complicate the main general themes. Painful though they may be, the conclusions that must be drawn from some of the failures of U.S. wishful thinking, and from some successes and unintended consequences, are too powerful and consistent to go away as foreign economic assistance is considered at a time of sharply limited resources.

1

The successes in this history have a common thread: *what was best achieved lay at ground zero relative to the overt purpose of the aid.* That is, whether the aim was economic or noneconomic, programs that were soundly designed and effectively administered were able to achieve *their most immediate goals.* It proved possible to give aid to build a dam and have the dam built. It proved possible to "pay rent" on a military base and then use the base.[1]

But distance from these overt, primary objectives reduced the likelihood of success and opened the door for increased unintended consequences. If the building of the dam is designed to provide power for a group of towns, that too can probably be accomplished. If the reason for doing *that* is to trigger an overall economic improvement in the region, the odds go down and the unpredictability is increased. If the reason for *that* (improving the entire economy of the region) is to make the governments of that region pro-U.S. liberal democracies, the connections get much less reliable. And if the ultimate goal is to make the *citizens* pro-U.S. liberal democrats, no one who reads this record can invest any serious hope in such a proposition.

Although important complexities must be introduced in the body of this report, they will not reduce the force of the call that history makes on U.S. policymakers, in both the administration and the Congress, to recognize that they should only decide to invest to build the dam if they are satisfied with the immediate result: getting the dam built. Achieving the immediate ends of such overseas assistance is difficult enough: this study demonstrates the risks of putting forward anything beyond the immediate goal as the reason for making the investment. But it recognizes that programs with multiple and noneconomic goals are still going to be manufactured and so charts a path with the best odds for success, noting the avoidable traps.

As Ernest Preeg's Philippine case study demonstrates, the *failure* to devise sound and achievable overt objectives and then maintain these objectives *as the entire content of our serious aspirations for what we intend the aid to accomplish* can lead to the result that *more harm than good is accomplished for overall U.S. objectives.* And, corollary to this, all the case studies demonstrate that extended political and security objectives *can be expected to undermine the achievement of the overt economic objectives.* The aid community in the United States has long argued for greater purity of purpose (i.e., sound economic goals only) in U.S. foreign assistance, and the study dramatizes why it feels this way. But the study also recognizes that objectives just as compelling as the "old" cold war objectives are already thrusting themselves upon policymakers and so examines the question of how best (and worst) to achieve noneconomic goals with these economic tools; there is little likelihood that policymakers will desist from trying. Indeed, the study recognizes that there have been important noneconomic successes in the past and, with proper strategy and execution, there can be in the future.

The case studies and additional cases informally surveyed confirm a consistent pattern of *potential effectiveness for economic assistance when the expectations, planning, execution, and overt goals of the aid are mutually consistent, along with a record of failed wishful thinking in cases not adhering to this discipline.*

The case studies and additional research touch frequently on the relationship between the donor's objectives and the recipient's objectives and predispositions. *Where the U.S. goal conflicted with interests of the recipient regime, or with its perception of those interests, or would have a significant impact on the political struggle between factions in the politics of the receiving country, chances of accomplishing the aid's purposes were steeply diminished.* The perceptions of ruling groups abroad may currently be undergoing some change as a result of the recently observed effects of prosperity on stability.

The findings also permit the formulation of important guidelines on whether aid can be anything more than a catalyst for political change, on economic objectives as facade for political intentions, on long-term versus short-term objectives for aid, on the phenomena created by having multiple goals for the same program, on "backlash," and on U.S. legislation.

And the guidelines below also indicate the advantages and disadvantages that can be expected from *cooperation with allies in foreign assistance* and how political impact and leverage can be maximized.

Although the scholars carrying out the case studies focused on the effectiveness of economic aid for achieving selected noneconomic objectives, they were consistently struck *by the damage these objectives inflicted on effective use, in economic terms, of the aid for its overt primary objectives.* This is a proper part of their analysis, because it is part of the cost of this use of aid and other kinds of economic assistance. The reader will find consistency in the impression that the cost was very high.

There is a discussion in chapter III of a pattern found in the case studies that is suggestive but for which the case studies offer insufficient evidence to label it a "finding." It points out that recipients of large amounts of aid, such as the Philippines and Pakistan, have poor economic growth and development records, while Mexico, a recipient only of assistance *other than* official aid, is currently doing remarkably well economically. This is suggestive and *significant* because of the likely search, under budget pressure, for modes of assistance in the future more similar to the help given Mexico than to official aid for the goal of economic development (as distinguished from humanitarian relief).

The political reality is that political and security purposes were often advanced as the reasons for economic assistance packages, especially if a credible link to the cold war offered itself. The fact that nothing as compelling as the cold war is likely to replace it raises legitimate concerns about the future of appropriations for foreign economic assistance coming from legislatures with the twin dogs of constituency politics and budget deficits snarling at their heels.

The question may come down to whether there is significant political support in the United States for some forms of humanitarian assistance, for international altruism. Even though the purposes of the aid are more likely to be achieved if they are not hidden behind other, more "marketable" goals, the political difficulty of coping with suffering abroad when there is suffering at home may cause leaders to continue to base aid requests on whatever rationale has the most domestic appeal.

A second possibility, of course, is that environmental concerns will take on the same urgency, with the same level of national consensus developing behind action and investment, that prevailed during the cold war. Nothing, however, in the action surrounding either the Rio Earth Summit or the early stages of the 1992 U.S. election suggests that Americans are near to this level of national accord and fervor.

But should saving the planet become a new absolutely central national crusade, the United States will face the same challenge defined by this study: avoiding unfounded hopes that generalized economic aid, or even good capital projects that are, nonetheless, unrelated to environmental action, can lead to desired behavior in a different sector. Will a generalized bribe to country X really induce it to protect its rain forest over the long run? Aid for the development and marketing of forest products might have a direct impact in the desired direction, but what response should be made to the country that claims simply that the level of economic desperation is too great to permit fancy environmental policies, that says "Cure the desperation and then we'll talk about the forest"?

This study suggests pessimism about cutting such a deal.

The Frozen Spigot

Another hard lesson for policymakers that emerges from this study is that *the effectiveness of U.S. influence over recipient-country action is in inverse proportion to the perceived importance that Washington attaches to the relationship.* If the receiving country believes that the spigot is frozen in the open position, that for reasons of strategic necessity or domestic politics it is not feasible for Washington to close the spigot, the influence the United States derives from the aid sinks close to zero. This piece of common sense is verified throughout the study, as is the Washington habit of acting as though the world did not operate that way.

No policymaker reading this evidence can avoid the necessity of having a *credible* hand on a turnable spigot in order to influence recipient-country action. *If the aim is economic reform and sustained development, Washington must be prepared to suspend aid if the receiving country falters in its commitment to the economic program that the aid is designed to support.* The U.S. government must be legally and

politically capable of turning down or turning off the flow of
assistance. One does not like to think of an unreliable flow
while, at the same time, suggesting that carefully conceived
capital projects have the best chance of success: they need
reliability of expectations, the ability to plan without mercurial
political meddling. The only way to avoid the tension between
these factors is to limit one's expectations about broad influence in the first place. The study clearly indicates the wisdom
of this course.

The spigot-leverage relationship is explored below in the
more detailed look at the findings. But the most general impli-
cation of the findings is that *the probability of success for U.S.
economic aid programs will vary enormously from country to
country.* Whether, however, the economic objective is easy or
difficult to attain, *achievement of the economic ends is more
likely than is achievement of the political or security ends
that are supposed to flow from the economic changes. It is
nonetheless possible to enhance the chances for success of the
latter. Of central importance in doing so is the factor of
leverage, which means that the aid should be conditioned on
the performance of the receiving country, with the flow of aid
credibly linked to realistic and well-understood performance
criteria.* A question could be raised about whether U.S.
policymakers really believed that they could work the changes
on Philippine or Pakistani economic performance that were
announced as the aid's aim. Whatever the case, politics, not
economics, clearly drove the process in the United States and
economic aid was perceived as useful for political purposes.
So it is striking that this general rule of what can be accomplished and what probably cannot be accomplished holds up
even in these cases. "Performance criteria" in the above
formulation is a factor usually attached to economic performance, but the rules of leverage are just as much at work in
noneconomic spheres.

The Guidelines

The headlines for policymakers announced above are among a
number of broad normative guidelines that the findings permit.
Behind them lies a set of conclusions that are likewise sup-

ported by (1) the four case studies carried out in this project,[1] (2) five studies of sub-Saharan African countries carried out in another CSIS project,[2] (3) a series of meetings with experts to grapple with the issues of what was general and what was particular in those studies, and (4) a review of the findings and an informal search for counterevidence, that is, for instances that appeared to cut across the tentative findings, carried out with the assistance of the all the regional study programs at the Center for Strategic and International Studies.

These findings go to the questions of why the strategy being examined—U.S. use of economic means for non-economic (i.e., security and political) purposes in the Third World—worked sometimes and sometimes did not. Specifically, the study looked at the relationship of the strategy and instruments of economic assistance to the pursuit of the noneconomic policy objectives of the United States (and some of its allies), especially national security, democratization, and international stability. What are the conditions, the goals, and the tactics most likely to lead to success or failure?

Despite the warnings contained in the headlines, the participants in the study, scholars and officials alike, believed that *there will be instances in the future when U.S. policymakers are attracted to the use of economic aid for non-economic purposes.*

But if Washington decides anew to taste this dangerous fruit, the study suggests that the U.S. government should pursue this strategy in a way radically different from that which has become traditional. Even taking all this good guidance about conditions, goals, and tactics into account, the achieving of the intended consequences is not certain, and the arrival on the doorstep of serious unintended consequences almost inevitable.

The fundamental message is, to use the instance above: only invest in the building of that dam if you will be satisfied with the existence of the dam, that and nothing more, as a payoff on the investment. But if the warning is not heeded, and Washington decides to build the dam in order to accomplish some further political and security objectives, the cases studied provide critical lessons for those making and imple-

menting the program. The one case where a long-term objective was stated early and then apparently achieved was the goal of Korean self-sufficiency as it related to the subsequent Korean "economic miracle" and the approach to (but not full achievement of) security self-sufficiency.

The question of cause-and-effect is treated in the Korea case study itself. But even in this case, the first lesson advanced by the author of the study is that "economic aid is a blunt, not subtle, tool." Further, in Korea certain slices of aid were targeted toward the goal of economic self-sufficiency with enough directness to make *this* the immediate goal (thereby also demonstrating that the immediacy of the goal and whether it is long-term or short-term are two different issues). Another key long-term goal in Korea was the fostering of democracy. But it was never the direct, immediate objective of any slice of the aid. The result was that, despite the size of the aid program, authoritarian government continued in Korea.

The findings also lead to the following conclusions:

• Even on a purely economic level, *we should not expect economic aid to be more than a catalyst. This is even more true where the goal is political change.* The real energy and commitment to improve economic performance must come from host-country leadership, local constituencies, and private investment. The role of aid, at best, *can* be to induce the receiving government to put its economic house in order and to foster an environment in which private enterprise can flourish. Even in the five sub-Saharan African countries studied, where aid donors succeeded in providing some impetus for economic reform, the driving force for *political* change came from inside the countries. (This lesson is all the more important in view of the modest size of the U.S. aid program in relation to the total resources needed by Third World economies.) The relationship here between the economic and noneconomic is fairly crude: the unleashing of market forces leads to the creation of a liberal and cosmopolitan middle class, which has proved to be dynamite for authoritarianism.

• The case studies do not indicate the impossibility of achieving some limited political or security objectives with aid from Washington. But where the desired political result is something more precise than that of the blunt relationship just described, the studies show that *if the main purpose is political, it is a mistake to devise elaborate economic objectives, pretending that these are the main purpose of the aid.*

• Many of the "new" noneconomic goals that may become part of the objectives of foreign assistance programs are, by nature, long-term. Although this is not the same as having goals that are secondary or part of a complex package of objectives, the *long-term character of these goals will create problems of (1) measurement of effectiveness and (2) maintenance of the pressure for recipient-country performance.* Nevertheless, aid will usually be long-term (Korean model), with occasional short-term instances (some Philippine examples). The critical finding of the study is that *where long- and short-term objectives occur together, the overall problem of multiple goals* (below) *is much exacerbated.* The tension between long-term goals (economic self-sufficiency, democracy, social reform) and short-term cold war goals in Pakistan became a serious drawback. (In the case of Pakistan, the case study author came to the conclusion that smaller amounts of economic assistance over a longer period, with a predictable disbursement pattern, would do more good than sudden infusions of larger sums.)

• On the question of cooperation with other donor countries, the study finds *advantages in the effectiveness of the political statement the aid makes and advantages in leverage if the aid flow is regulated by an international agency with a reputation for toughness in relating recipient-country performance to spigot-control. An informal consortium or mere parallel individual-country giving tend to **diminish** leverage,* for reasons discussed in the last chapter. The United States is capable of improving the probability of effectiveness of any multiple-donor initiative by taking the lead in organizing for the policy objectives among all the aid donors and urging each to make its own aid conditional upon appropriate behavior by the recipient.

• Although the case studies focused on the attempt to accomplish noneconomic ends through the means of economic assistance, the *backlash* of the initiatives studied became an important part of the story in all cases. There is a consistent pattern of *jeopardizing the achievement of the principal stated economic goals by the presence of other, noneconomic goals.* The Philippine case study finds that the priority given to noneconomic objectives distorted and damaged the economic program and prevented support for some sectors of the program. (The author predicts that if aid to the Philippines continues to be linked, or even to be *perceived* to be linked, to noneconomic objectives, U.S. trade and investment will lose ground to donors not making the same mistake.) The history of the U.S.-Pakistan aid relationship is also one of the economic value of aid being limited because of noneconomic objectives. This consistent finding explains the antagonism of much of the aid community toward program objectives that damage "their" priorities. But the point is crucial because of the importance that economic performance is likely to have among aid objectives of the future.

So a striking conclusion of the research is not just the difficulty and unlikelihood of achieving secondary and tertiary objectives, objectives not immediate to the exact aid given, but *the strongly deleterious effect of these "other" objectives on the accomplishing of the economic objectives (including those of commercial consequence).* Powerfully dramatized by Ernest Preeg's study, this factor is present in all the cases.

An interesting phenomenon found in the studies is that of *reverse damage,* the instances in which economic reform and progress work counter to such political objectives as stability. The Mexican case suggests that this is mainly a *short-term* phenomenon.

• The factors of damage to the accomplishment of economic objectives, and short-term reverse damage, are really just sub-sets of a larger, very consistent, finding in the case studies, the additional African cases, and the review by CSIS regional study programs: the presence of *multiple objectives of any kind for the same program of economic assistance sharply reduces the chances for achieving all but the most immediate primary goal, and will inflict at least some damage on that primary effort also.* The Mexican study suggests that Washington had not thought out systematically the relationship between its economic strategy and the achievement of its noneconomic objectives. In Korea, U.S. officials are found expressing confusion about which group of goals had priority. In the Philippines, the multiple objectives that got in each other's way were even on the same side of "the line" (between the economic and the noneconomic): the linkage to base rights adversely affected political objectives. At times when Washington's strategic interest in Pakistan has been at one of its high points, the United States has failed to use economic assistance effectively to achieve other goals. Gen. Graves's judgment on the basis of the five African studies is that "donors intent on supporting both a transition to democratic government and economic policy reform will face the dilemma of whether to give priority to the political survival of the fledgling government or to economic change. In aid programs political and economic objectives have often been . . . in conflict."[3]

• The *leverage-spigot* relationship is summarized in a special section above. Put simply, *leverage to affect the reforms, policies, and other behavior of the receiving country is directly tied to the credibility of the donor's ability and willingness (legal, administrative, and political) to regulate the flow of aid in response to recipient performance.* This factor operates with special intensity and complexity in the case of an economic assistance program with multiple goals, a phenomenon treated in the next point.

In Korea, the leverage over recipient policies was *minimized* during the Syngman Rhee period because withholding aid would have jeopardized objectives that were perceived (correctly) by the Koreans as having an extremely high priority in Washington. Specifically, Seoul knew that the primary U.S. goal was to advance its own position in the cold war in the short run, and so Korean leaders reasoned that the goal of democratization was postponable without any (believable) risk that Washington would react at the spigot. Over the course of about 40 years of U.S. grant assistance there was no enduring progress toward real democracy, despite all the U.S. efforts. If U.S. assistance helped promote some of the economic conditions that in turn produced the social conditions that in turn produced the political conditions for the recent movement

toward democratization, that outcome is very different from
any serious Korean response to the paper tiger of U.S. pressure
during the earlier period. Democratization is occurring now,
when Korea's dependence on U.S. aid has ended. (The point on
the predispositions of the recipient country's ruling factions,
also explored in this section of the report, was also in play in
our inability to force or induce political reforms.)

The credibility of the hand on the spigot can also be weakened by confusion over the level of aid or the factors that will
affect it, as is seen in the Philippine case. And in this case, so
long as Manila thought that the Americans simply *had* to
retain the military bases, they could ignore any threats about
delay or suspension of assistance on this or other topics. The
aid could be disbursed as political patronage, ignoring the
objective of democratic reform. These relationships were so
clear that the Communists could portray the United States as
being under the thumb of *Marcos's* leverage. The intention of
Washington policymakers and legislators that U.S. support
would lead to both economic and political reform was frus-
trated because the leverage was missing. The single noneconomic objective (the bases) damaged everything else. Even
with the change of regime, the aid given to show political
support for Corazon Aquino had so little perceived relation to
either Philippine needs or performance that it carried no
leverage for economic reform and functioned only as a crude
one-time statement of political support, unrelated to genuine
leverage to influence future events.

In Pakistan, everything that enhanced the perceived importance of Pakistan in Washington's regional security strategy
reduced spigot-credibility and leverage. The Soviet invasion of
Afghanistan destroyed the remaining shreds of credibility for
the idea that Washington would actually suspend or delay the
aid flow in response to Pakistani performance on other aid
objectives. Note that the Soviet withdrawal from Afghanistan
was followed by a freeze on aid; the Pakistani calculation had
been correct. The period when all goals other than Pakistan's
cooperation on Afghanistan were secondary had ended.

• The factor of multiple goals is, in some of the cases,
linked to that of spigot-control to create the worst possible

situation for exerting leverage on the recipient. *If one or some of the goals of a multiple-goal program are seen as vitally important to the United States, leverage is destroyed relative to all the other goals; if it is not credible that the United States will turn off the spigot because it attaches so much importance to X, the recipient has no reason to heed Washington's demands on any of the other objectives.*

• All cases and associated research underscore *the importance of the relationship between the donor's objectives and those of the recipient country.* This rather obvious point is given its proper complications by the cases: when speaking of "the recipient country" what really counts is the *ruling group's perception* of those interests. Within this, the cases point to the ruling group's perceptions of *its own, not the country's, interests,* and of the *development of counter-constituencies* for the aid if it, or the conditions it would promote, are seen as a threat to any of the significant competitors in the internal struggle for power. Although taking these predispositions into account would seem to be a prudent calculation that all policymakers would undertake, the cases reveal that Washington has frequently missed this step, or had the political ground shift under its feet (in ways that should not, however, have caused surprise). What should not be ignored in the future is the need to *design aid programs to provide results that will be advantageous (and be perceived to be advantageous) to both Washington and the recipient,* recognizing that "the recipient" might mean several factions powerful enough to control the success or failure of the aid.

Account must be taken of other donors of economic assistance. This means more than the logical relationships among the programs, their ends, and their procedures. It means also understanding and planning strategy around the constituencies that are affected by, even developed by, the aid programs of other donors. The tangled history of the interplay of multiple donors in the same recipient country would afford interesting analysis but probably few generalizations to guide policymakers on subsequent occasions, beyond the admonition that, in most cases, the United States is not alone.

In general the case studies illustrate that where the interests of the recipient country and the noneconomic goals of the United States coincided, such use of U.S. economic aid successfully accomplished its purpose. Both the donor and recipient benefited. When, however, the U.S. goal conflicted with the interests of the administration of the recipient country or threatened the existence of that group, U.S. economic aid failed to accomplish its foreign policy purpose. Especially was this true if the national security objective of the United States in the recipient country was known to be of high priority to the United States. In the case of Korea, U.S. economic aid was a source of the patronage that helped to keep Syngman Rhee in power; it was therefore important to him. The same was true of Ferdinand Marcos in the Philippines. In each country the granting of human rights and ending of oppression would have threatened the existence of the strongman; no progress was made by the United States toward the goal of democracy and in fact the United States did not push rigorously. In each country, moreover, U.S. threats to withdraw aid were not credible; the recipient knew that the prime U.S. goal was advancing its own position in the cold war in the short run and that democratization as a goal was postponable.[4] In fact, bargaining power lay with the recipient, not with the aid donor. In contrast to Syngman Rhee, who had no real interest in the economy of his country or in development aid per se, Park Chung Hee decided early in his tenure that "long-term U.S. sponsorship was no longer guaranteed."[5] He rejected the "calculated dependence of the Rhee years," and sought greater economic and military independence from the United States. In other words, U.S. and Korean goals as donor and recipient coincided. The consequence was an improvement in bilateral relations and, within a decade, the end of U.S. economic aid and the start of the Korean economic miracle. The long-term U.S. goals of putting Korea into a position of being able to maintain a strong defense force and operate at an acceptable level of living without U.S. aid were accomplished; democratization, however, was still a hope for the future.

The case studies are replete with instances where the predisposition of politically powerful factions, including the country's ruling group, were pivotal and, when push came to shove, were not shoved out of the way by the will of the donor. Moving to a market economy in Mexico interfered with the subsidies received by favored constituencies. Many of the new governments in sub-Saharan Africa owe their rise to power to constituencies that benefit from the status quo and would be damaged by economic reform. Failure to achieve human rights goals in Korea stemmed from the threat this constituted to Syngman Rhee, as did any moves toward democracy, another goal imposed on the aid program. In Mexico, the overall threat affecting Mexican predispositions came from the idea that an economy based on individual initiative might undermine the authoritarian civic culture. The Philippine government went all the way in defending the difference between its and Washington's goals when it demanded rent-labeled-as-rent for the military bases, freeing it to use the money for its own purposes.

On occasion, mixing into internal politics has been an important (though seldom advertised) part of U.S. objectives, well beyond such simple formulations as the promotion of democratization. One reason for Washington's interest in the establishment of a functioning market economy in Mexico is the hope that this would discredit the policy prescriptions of the Mexican Left. In fact, the Mexican case study shows that the measure of consensus achieved on economic policy has moderated the extreme Left and also undermined the scare tactics of the far Right. In such cases, the relationship between the aid and internal political factions was deliberate.

- *The study does not provide decisive support for the idea of rewriting the Foreign Assistance Act.* One could undertake to write new legislation in order to limit strictly the purposes for which aid may be provided—and do so reading the lessons of this study—but the legislative chances for a major revision are unclear, and once started down that road in the Congress, the finishing point is unpredictable. Among participants in the study were admirers of the Hamilton-Gilman report but also those with strong questions about the wisdom of trying to dictate all the purposes of aid in a piece of general legislation.

- Because of the slices of history studied, the noneconomic objectives were mostly cold war-related security and political goals. *But neither the case studies nor the experts involved in the study suggest that the lessons learned are confined to those particular noneconomic objectives.* The same mistakes could be made in efforts with other non-economic ends in view, from narcotics control to environmental protection.

• The Korean case study makes an interesting case for striving for public, rather than government, support for aid objectives. Because this was the only study to focus on *public diplomacy* as a factor in the strategic thinking relative to economic assistance, the discussion in that case study cannot properly be called a finding or recommendation of the project as a whole. But it is suggestive of paths to follow in subsequent work.

In the final section an attempt is made to put together the principal characteristics of a foreign assistance program with the best odds for success, according to the study's findings. The central conclusion is that the best odds obtain when the *objective is economic; closely related to* (or exactly the same as) *the specific work to be carried out by the aid project; short-term; genuinely supported by the political leadership* of the recipient country; *not burdened with secondary objectives;* and disbursed, delayed, or suspended according to a *credible and tight connection to the donor's insistence on clear performance standards,* whether the donor is the United States alone, the United States and its allies, or an international agency.

The Case Findings

Korea

Aid to Korea, which, according to much of the rhetoric, was intended to foster democracy, left Korea with an authoritarian government.[1] But the political leadership of East Asia is learning that with prosperity comes the formation of a middle class, and a middle class is a threat to dictatorship. If Korea arrives at stable democracy, and U.S. aid was an important part of the early mix that kept the Korean economy from collapsing under the burden of the Korean War, then one might judge that the U.S. strategy worked. Korea proves to be, however, not so much a countercase as a demonstration of the need to think in terms of four levels of consequence relative to aid given:

- The immediate consequences that the aid is explicitly designed to accomplish. These will be economic except when the political or security goal has been made overt, as when one or both governments call military base rental by its proper name.
- The intended secondary consequences, in which the aid donor believes that by achieving the first level of consequences, this second level will flow as a result. Here we find most of the political and security goals of the post-war period, and here we find most of the disappointment, most of the illusions, most of the disillusionment.
- The long-term consequences which may parallel either of the first two levels, but did not come about in the direct cause-and-effect manner intended by the donor. If, for example, democracy and security come to Korea through student-led rebellion and a change in the North Korean threat, they might not constitute an endorsement of the original vision of the aid donor.
- The unintended consequences.

In Korea, the route to some of the changes in Korea's political life is very distant from that envisaged by the U.S. optimists who designed the programs. The factors involved, reviewed below, are instructive and consistent with other cases.

The Philippines

Aid to the Philippines in the period studied in this research—1979 to 1991—had explicit security and political objectives. The security objectives were so important to the United States, and the Philippine government became so secure in the belief that Washington would not dare to interfere with the disbursements, that the political objective of democratization could languish and even the declared economic aims became orphans to which neither government was seriously committed. At the end of the period, the arrival of Corazon Aquino in the presidency triggered a fresh belief that economic aid from Washington would reform the Philippine economy and strengthen democracy. Ambassador Preeg's compelling case study shows the factors that caused this aid actually to undermine the incentive for economic reform and to bolster some of the most retrograde forces in Philippines political life. His study has already made an enlightened contribution to the aid debate on the floor of the Congress.

Pakistan

The Pakistan case study shows cold war considerations dominating the provision of aid and economic assistance always complementing military assistance. The level of economic assistance fluctuated, not with the pace of progress along agreed economic paths, but according to U.S. strategic interest in cooperation with Pakistan; the Pakistanis surely saw that their performance in the use of the aid was not the determining factor in the spigot action. This case illustrates dramatically the formula noted above: the greater the strategic interest of the United States, as perceived by Pakistan, the less effective the efforts to use economic assistance to further such goals as reducing drug trafficking, promoting democracy and human rights, forestalling nuclear proliferation, and fostering economic reform.

In Pakistan the other main lesson for policymakers is seen with stark clarity: economic assistance motivated by security and political considerations is of limited value as an agent of economic development and social and political reform.

Mexico

Mexico, a controversial subject for a case study at the beginning of the project because of the form of the assistance given (primarily debt relief and trade concessions), proved valuable in the end as a demonstration that some of the factors found in the other studies were not unique to official economic assistance, broadening the value of the findings for the future (given the probability of tight limits on conventional aid because of budget constraints).

A positive feature of the Mexican relationship, compared with the other cases, is the relatively high priority given to economic objectives in both the overt and the "real" motives of Washington policymakers. This does not mean that the

Mexican case is somehow outside the cold war context of the
other cases. As Delal Baer writes:

> In the modern era, containment implied countering Cuban
> and Soviet involvement in the domestic battles of Latin
> nations. . . Mexico's revolutionary legacy led it to pursue
> relations with the Soviet bloc that have often been to the
> detriment of U.S. security objectives in the region. The
> Soviet and Cuban embassies have long been disproportion-
> ate in size to their trade and consular missions, serving as
> espionage centers. Soviet efforts to establish consular offices
> in the Baja California peninsula prompted vociferous U.S.
> protests, given the sensitive military installations located in
> San Diego. Similarly, Mexico hosted the headquarters of
> Central American guerrilla groups and acted diplomatically
> to frustrate U.S. efforts to contain and reverse Sandinista
> activities.[2]

None of this was absent from the minds of U.S. policymakers
as they worked on the various forms of assistance extended to
the Mexican economy.

That economic modernization can be expected to have an
impact on politics is clear to all, but there was relatively less
wishful thinking driving U.S. decision making in the Mexican
case. The case shows the interesting relationship between
economic consensus and political consensus among the citizens of the receiving country, useful for future calculations,
but, in general, technicolor political and security hopes did not
drive U.S. strategy here.

The Study

This report grew out of research supported by the Pew Charitable Trusts and was undertaken at CSIS on the use of U.S.
economic aid to achieve noneconomic foreign policy objectives.

For some years the Pew Trusts have been interested in the
relation between economics and national security, sponsoring
a variety of projects at research institutions on aspects of this
subject. At CSIS, Pew-sponsored research involved examining
in detail the use of tools of economic assistance by the U.S.
government to pursue political and strategic goals in four

recipient countries: Mexico, Pakistan, the Philippines, and South Korea. Additional evidence from a CSIS study of related issues in five sub-Saharan African countries was also used. As noted, the study looked at the relationship of the strategy and instruments of economic assistance to the pursuit of the noneconomic policy objectives of United States (and some of its allies) especially national security, democratization, and international stability. The study also assessed the past effectiveness and prospective utility of various means of allied cooperation in extending economic assistance to achieve these objectives.

The case-study countries were chosen because the United States had important and diverse noneconomic policy goals in each, because documentation was plentiful, and because CSIS had notable strengths for research in those regions. As the work unfolded, the selection of countries looked increasingly felicitous. Although Korea had the difficulty that the principal aid effort was well into the past, this gave the best opportunity for a fair assessment of the long-term effects of the aid. Although the assistance given to Mexico was in forms other than official economic assistance, this gave insight into which of the factors discovered in the other case studies were confined only to traditional aid and which might be generalized to include other forms of support and assistance. The problem was not the presence of Mexico in the study, but that there was only *one* Mexico; the pattern found there should be the starting point of some interesting analysis.

Much of the research design came from meetings with those policymakers and their staffs who are the natural audience for this report. They helped determine what should be asked of each case. Colleagues from Pew were active participants in some of these sessions. The donor played an unusual role as an active intellectual participant throughout the early stages, accepting, and being willing to wrestle with, the risks and difficulties throughout.

The first draft of each case study was reviewed by a CSIS team and, after revision, by a panel of outside experts who had agreed to review the draft critically. In the case of the study of the Philippines, CSIS was urged by both administration and

Hill officials to publish immediately because the issues addressed in the case study were at the center of current policy debate. The study's findings were *already* the subject of discussion in Washington, as was true of others of the case studies, because there had been no request to the participating outside experts about maintaining confidentiality. Somewhat reluctantly, because the full import of the case is best seen in the context of the overall study, CSIS published the Philippines study in its Significant Issues Series.

Full texts of all the case studies and of the African study are available from the CSIS Publications Office.

The Historical Moment

It was decisively important for the political significance of this study that it was launched as the Berlin Wall fell and the Soviet Empire unraveled. The end of the cold war means a necessary rethinking of the political engine behind much of U.S. foreign economic assistance over the last 40 years. The study, even if the timing was more fortuitous than calculated, offers itself as the logical starting place for that rethinking.

With the shadow of the superpower rivalry removed, we can see more clearly those other dangers and opportunities for which aid might be an effective instrument—if the lessons of recent history are understood and heeded. Global and regional stability are now threatened by poverty, the maldistribution of resources, disease, the narcotics trade, ethnic strife, the abuse of human rights, mass migration, nuclear proliferation and the spread of other weapons of mass destruction and, long range, environmental degradation. This array of threats will constitute a drain on, perhaps the exhaustion of, the resources and vitality of the international system. The resources that were thrown, often on the basis of guesswork and wishful thinking, at cold war objectives will not be available to the United States and its allies in the future.

And there are also the unrealized opportunities. Despite the political earthquake of the last three years, neither market-based free enterprise nor Western-style pluralistic government has been installed as the worldwide pattern.

The historical context is one that demands a far more stringent relationship between reality and goals, and then between goals and investment, than that to which cold war policymakers were accustomed.

During the cold war, the United States used economic and security assistance as major policy instruments in its rivalry with the Soviet Union. Three of the four case studies reported on below describe situations dominated by cold war concerns; and the citation above from Dr. Baer's study of Mexico dramatizes the high importance of cold war factors even in that case. The cases show, as does the history we all know, that various combinations of such assistance made a major contribution to the success of the Western alliance and the maintenance of the U.S. position in several corners of the earth.

In many cases economic assistance was used in the pursuit of noneconomic objectives, bolstered either by apparently tight reasoning or by obvious wishful thinking in the connection asserted between the aid and its goals. It has been, and remains, a controversial concept.

But it is one that will continue to offer itself to policymakers. Wherever we have relative wealth and no easy direct path to achieving desired political and security goals, the idea that maybe an investment of this kind will pay off is going to spring to mind. If it does not, the potential recipient countries will find ways to suggest it. The response, if it is to be more than guesswork (and a fresh supply of wishful thinking), must be based on analysis of what works, what does not, and under what conditions.

The case studies and their context in history show how often Washington turned to economic aid as a cold war weapon. Foreign aid is still considered to be a useful foreign policy tool by official Washington, even with the end of the cold war. But in all the ferment of new ideas being offered for revising the goals of the aid programs, few in either the executive or legislative branches have suggested using economic aid solely for purposes of improving the economic conditions and performance in receiving countries. That is the stark context of this study.

Part Two
Analysis

Context and Cases: History, Politics and Concepts in U.S. Foreign Aid

The U.S. foreign assistance program has changed considerably in size and composition over the decades of its existence, whether its origin is dated to 1946 to include the Marshall Plan, as is the practice of some analysts, or to the beginning of aid for economic development (as opposed to aid for reconstruction) in the early 1950s, or to the creation of an integrated aid agency in the early 1960s as the U.S. Agency for International Development (USAID) itself does.

In terms of purchasing power, the real value of aid expenditures has declined since the Marshall Plan and Korean War period. More of the available assistance has taken the form of grants, while loans have become a smaller share of the total, especially during the 1980s. At the same time military aid (and other categories related to military purposes) has waxed and waned as a share of the total for assistance for purposes of economic development (and related uses such as relief) in response to variations in the temperature of the cold war. Military assistance and the Economic Support fund combined have amounted to more than half of the annual U.S. foreign assistance program since the late 1960s. Charts 1 and 2 illustrate these trends.

In the main, these shifts are a reflection of the extension of the cold war in the early 1950s into the Third World arena and its intensification there. They also mirror the increasing importance of the Middle East as an area of national security concern starting with the oil crisis of the 1970s. The end of the cold war in the early 1990s has effectively eliminated the main raison d'être (at least in the public rhetoric of its supporters) for the U.S. foreign aid program as it has existed for the past 40 years.

In what follows, chapter I examines the primacy of the national security motive for economic aid and undertakes to explain that primacy.[1] Chapter II examines economic aid as an instrument of national security policy; it seeks examples of

Chart 1
U.S. Economic and Military Assistance Programs,
Fiscal Years 1946–1992
(in constant 1992 billion U.S. dollars)

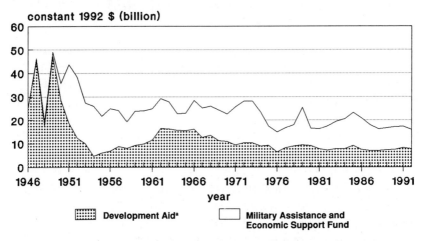

Source: Plotted from U.S. Agency for International Development data, courtesy of Larry Nowels, Congressional Research Service, Library of Congress, Washington, D.C.

[a]Includes food aid, Development Assistance, other bilateral assistance, contributions to MDBs (multilateral development organizations).

Chart 2
Loans and Grants as a Percentage of Total U.S. Aid,
Fiscal Years 1946–1990

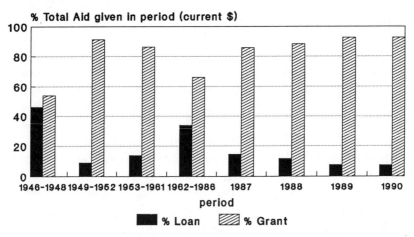

Source: Developed from data from U.S. Overseas Loans and Grants, U.S. Agency for International Development, Washington, D.C., 1991.

both the subordination of other economic and political purposes to the security goal and of the primacy of other motives
over the security motive. It examines the conditions under
which economic aid has successfully accomplished its goal and
seeks trends in its effectiveness. Chapter III expands upon the
more general recommendations and guidelines already previewed in the opening pages of this report.

Chapter I
The Primacy of the National Security Purpose of Aid

Dr. Penelope Hartland-Thunberg, who provided this study with the literature search that gave it its academic context (and prevented duplication of effort), has looked at the history of postwar assistance with an eye particularly to national security objectives. This chapter is about beginnings. More recent developments are not examined, nor is the other side of the struggle for aid funds—the development and humanitarian objectives. Tracing the latter group of objectives would mean telling the story of the Alliance for Progress initiative of the 1960s, the Basic Human Needs strategy of the 1970s, the Caribbean Basin Initiative of the early 1980s, and the Africa Fund approach of the mid-1980s. The fact is that some of these U.S. initiatives seem more distant to the current political moment than do some of the security-led efforts that had, historically, an earlier beginning. In the near future, whether we like it or not, there is more likely to be assistance related to, for example, hopes about Middle East security than a new Alliance for Progress. This is not the case for policy-conditioned cash transfers and direct support for the private sector. The phrase to watch, and for which this study will be useful, is "policy-conditioned." In each case, the question will have to be asked about the objectives of the initiative and the strategy relative to those objectives. This study suggests how important the answers to those questions will be.

The following is Dr. Thunberg's sketch of these developments.

The swings in U.S. bilateral relations with South Korea, the Philippines, Pakistan, and Mexico have been dominated by national security and other noneconomic foreign policy considerations. This has been especially true of U.S. aid policies and practices in these countries, as the case studies abundantly document. Time and again, the use of aid for purposes of economic development, democratization, or political stability in these countries was subordinated to perceived U.S.

national security urgencies. The overall history suggests that these case studies are representative and reflect the rule rather than the exception in U.S. aid motives.

U.S. foreign economic aid was one in a series of bold, forward-thinking, innovative foreign policy initiatives of the United States in the early post–World War II years. These initiatives were often directed toward eliminating prewar practices and institutions that had produced political instability around the world and finally war.[1] The motive in every case was to support the ultimate U.S. national security and foreign policy objectives—world peace and freedom; the economic aid program was one of the policy instruments employed toward this end.

For the past half-century there has been considerable misunderstanding of the reasons for U.S. economic aid. It was generally not extended for purposes of economic development abroad; from the beginning economic growth in the less developed countries (LDCs) was mandated as the means of buttressing U.S. national security interests, not as an end in itself.[2] In fact, the great bulk of foreign aid has been politically motivated although the distinction between political and economic motivations becomes blurred when economic development is perceived to contribute directly to U.S. national security goals.

The Early History of Aid's Objectives

The pre-1960 history of the U.S. economic aid program throws some light on the origins of the primacy of national security considerations in the use of U.S. economic aid. This is not the place to review the full history of the aid program, but rather to establish that, before the birth of the aid agency in 1961, there was no golden age when economic aid was mandated solely for the purpose of economic development. The 1961 legislation stated unequivocally in its preamble that its purpose was to promote "the foreign policy, security and general welfare of the United States."[3] Although that legislation has been frequently amended since 1961, the preamble remains the same. Many of the amendments have added to the objectives of the legislation more specifics, mostly political, about the goals of the program.[4] Thus, in the three decades since

1960 the law has clearly stated that economic aid has existed to serve the foreign policy and welfare interests of the United States. In the 1940s and 1950s, however, there were various pieces of legislation concerned in some way with foreign economic aid. They, too, sought to promote the national security of this country.

During the entire post–World War II era, of course, many considerations have motivated members of the executive branch, the legislative branch, and the electorate to support or oppose a foreign economic aid program. Many in Congress and the administration supported legislation whose stated purpose was to promote U.S. national security because they believed that only for this reason would the entire Congress vote in favor of a foreign economic aid program. Their main objective, however—their own private agenda—was aid for humanitarian purposes, because helping to alleviate poverty was a moral obligation. Another group supported foreign aid for the opposite reason—because it did promote national security despite the fact that there were equally needy causes at home.

In general, two basic philosophies have motivated the supporters of foreign economic aid. One has been moral and idealistic: It is the *right* thing to do; those who have should share with those who have not. The other has been pragmatic: it is in the U.S. self-interest; the United States cannot exist as an island of plenty in a sea of poverty. Idealists supported economic aid for purposes of economic development: for the pragmatists that was not enough; aid must primarily benefit the United States. President Harry S. Truman fell into the first group in his public utterances, although at least as early as March 1947, he recognized the interdependence between political and economic relations. In a speech at Baylor University, Truman commented, "Our foreign relations, political and economic, are indivisible."[5] In other words there is no foreign policy issue that is purely a political or an economic one—or a security issue; every foreign policy issue contains elements of each.

Media people and most academics who concerned themselves with such issues were also among the idealists. The Congress and a good part of the electorate fell into the second group, the pragmatists. In addition there were always those who looked askance at foreign aid, viewing it at best as a global dole, sometimes as a total waste.

The influence of the idealists, the pragmatists, and the opponents of aid has varied through the near-half-century of U.S. aid programs. The idealists' strength peaked in the 1950s when committed and articulate writers like Barbara Ward, writing in *The Economist,* and the sociologist Gunnar Myrdal in Sweden captured much attention and support. They and others like them argued eloquently for increasing foreign aid to relieve poverty in the Third World because it was right to do so. Even in the 1950s, however, the idealists never captured the U.S. Congress to the extent that their priorities became those of the Congress. Nevertheless, their influence on some members was important, and for many humanitarian objectives gave an additional reason to support aid packages, even if they were not the decisive objectives.

From the earliest appearance of the precursors to the integrated economic development program that was first legislated in 1961, U.S. economic aid was principally mandated by the Congress as an instrument in the cold war, to support our allies—actual or potential—in building their economic strength while coping with the necessity for defense expenditures to protect themselves *and us* itself from the threat of Communist aggression or subversion. The Truman administration was strongly motivated by the urgency of blocking the gains of the Communist parties in Western Europe where wartime destruction enforced very austere living conditions. Something had to be done. That something, the Marshall Plan, was viewed in the 1950s—improperly—as a precursor of aid to developing countries.[6]

Economic aid as a transfer of resources on concessionary terms was conceived in the early post–World War II years as a means of ensuring peace and political stability in the developing world. It is true that British writers trace foreign aid to the budgetary support (often termed grants-in-aid) given by nineteenth-century colonial powers to their colonies.[7] Even they, however, agree that aid as a concessionary transfer between sovereign states emerged from the ferment of innovative ideas

that characterized the Truman postwar era in the United
States.

The idea of economic aid was first articulated by Secretary
of State George Marshall in a commencement address at
Harvard University in June 1947.[8] In his speech, Marshall
stressed that economic reconstruction in Europe would take
much longer than originally envisaged, that shortages were
pervasive throughout the European economy and inflation
everywhere a threat. His only statement about the motive for
U.S. assistance was: "It is logical that the U.S. should do whatever it is able to do to assist in the return of normal economic
health in the world, without which there can be no political
stability and no assured peace."[9] The foreign policy and national security justification for aid to Europe, embodied in the
concluding clause, is clearly a *va sans dire* appendage.
Marshall's obvious idealism may have been diluted during the
speech-clearing process by a cautious pragmatist someplace in
the administration.

The subsequent Marshall Plan (1948–1952) legislation was
debated and passed in remarkably short order by the Congress[10] but not without probing questions from the members,
including that of what would happen in Europe if the aid
proposal were not enacted. The program was justified by its
supporters in terms of saving U.S. defense expenditures by
rebuilding Western Europe's strength in order that the United
States might have a partner in confronting Soviet aggression.[11]

The concept of economic aid to support economic growth
(as opposed to supporting reconstruction) was extended to the
developing countries by President Truman in his inaugural
address to the Congress in January 1949. The fourth proposal
in his program for peace and freedom in the world (the subtitle
of his speech was "False Philosophy of Communism") was for
an economic development program (later called the "Point IV
program") involving a partnership of business, labor, agriculture, and government in many countries to reduce poverty in
the developing world.[12]

Even before Truman's Point IV speech, however, the
subject of emergency aid for developing countries was forced
on the president and the Congress in the spring of 1947 by

requests from Greece and Turkey for financial, economic, and expert aid in reconstruction and development. Included in the request was aid for the government in obtaining from abroad "the means of restoring . . . [the] security indispensable to the achievement of economic and political recovery."[13] Both countries were facing a serious challenge from Communist insurgencies. The Congress expressed many doubts about the request, questioning whether intervention was in the U.S. national interest. The legislation mandating the aid clearly stated in the preamble its importance to the national security of the United States.[14]

Although Truman's 1949 Point IV proposal aimed at a broadly based goal of economic development, the actual program that emerged from the Congress the following year was modest. It provided for technical assistance to developing countries and verbal encouragement to private capital investment there. Iran, Ceylon, Brazil, Liberia, India, Korea, and the Philippines all eventually received technical assistance through the Point IV program.

Also in 1949, in the Mutual Defense Act authorizing *military* aid, the Congress went out of its way to acknowledge the importance of *economic* aid:

> [T]he Congress also recognizes that economic recovery is essential to international peace and security and must be given clear priority. The Congress also recognizes that the increased confidence of free peoples in their ability to resist direct or indirect aggression and to maintain internal security will advance such recovery and political stability.[15]

The Congress as well as the president recognized the blurred distinction between economic and security policies.

This theme was restated continuously in Truman's speeches and those of the top officials of the State Department and the foreign aid agencies throughout his administration. For example: "the Point IV Program is not just a program to 'do good.' It is very clearly a program in our own self-interest."[16]

After the Korean War (1950–1953), during which 30,000 U.S. lives were lost, a program of economic and military aid for Korea was perceived as essential to ensure that U.S. troops could return home and stay there.[17] Military assistance began in 1950 except for minute amounts in the late 1940s. Once again, strengthening U.S. national security was the consideration that fostered congressional support for the aid initiative.

Aid programs for Philippine and Korean economic development were among the first sustained U.S. efforts to support economic growth in a developing country. Like their precursors, these developmental aid programs and their successors were perceived as an instrument of U.S. national security policy, a means of containing the spread of communism, first in Asia along the Communist periphery and then in other parts of the world. Mosley notes that in the mid-1950s three-quarters of U.S. aid commitments were concentrated in Asia.[18]

During the early postwar years, President Truman urged expanded foreign aid appropriations on the country, stating that the program was necessary to U.S. national security but also because it was the right thing to do. In his July 1951 economic report, Truman discussed the security and economic reasons for U.S. foreign aid efforts, adding "[t]he moral aspects of this issue are even more important than the economic. The great need of the twentieth century is to achieve a steadily improving morality to keep pace with growing technology."[19]

In contrast to Truman's idealism, President Dwight D. Eisenhower (1952–1960) showed little interest in economic development. Foreign aid was continued and expanded during his administration, but the new programs were undertaken to contain communism (Vietnam) or to reduce "heavy" U.S. agricultural surpluses (PL 480).[20] During the 1950s, to be sure, domestic economic problems captured most of the president's attention, first because of the strong inflationary consequences of the Korean War and then later in the decade because of the developing deficit in the U.S. balance of payments. During his first term, however, neither President Eisenhower nor his Council of Economic Advisers (CEA) made any mention of aid or the developing countries in their annual economic reports, in stark contrast to their predecessors, who devoted at least several paragraphs to the subject every year, addressing both the pragmatic and the idealistic reasons for foreign aid. During the second Eisenhower term, the CEA briefly mentioned the reason for the Mutual Security Program as enabling other countries to "make the military effort needed in the common interest"; and finally (in the very last report of Eisenhower's CEA), assistance to the developing countries was stated to have "retained its high priority."[21] Unenthusiastic pragmatism, at best.

Regardless of presidential idealism or pragmatism, however, the Congress remained reluctant to vote for economic aid for development's sake; rather, money was appropriated to strengthen U.S. national security by buttressing democratic forces and freedom around the world through rising standards of living. Congressional pragmatists remained immune to idealism.

In 1959 the Draper report, responding to the president's request for a "critical appraisal . . . of the relative emphasis which should be given to military and economic programs, particularly in the less developed areas," observed: "It is obvious that, but for the communist threat, appropriations of the size thus far made for our assistance programs . . . would not have been possible."[22] Economic and military aid, in other words, were viewed as complementary tools in the effort by the United States to bolster its national security against the hostile force of communism.

In academia, meanwhile, the idea of foreign aid was enthusiastically received. Among anthropologists, sociologists, economists, and others, academia's enthusiasm for aid was almost exclusively for aid to be used for purposes of economic development and rising standards of living in the Third World, especially among those at the bottom of the income scale. Political scientists explored the relations between economic development and democratization while recognizing that politically united people are less likely to be the object of external aggression and more likely to participate constructively in the world community. Most academics seemed to share President Truman's idealism and a belief that helping people to rise out of poverty was morally correct, the right thing to do. Many explicitly regretted that U.S. aid was granted for "selfish" motives. Because aid was not extended solely for economic purposes, this group believed, its effectiveness in alleviating poverty was weakened while the national security of the United States was not notably strengthened. Some became increasingly strident in their criticisms of the aid program because they failed to recognize the reasons for its origin.

In fact, it seems to have been only the political scientists who recognized that economic aid was mandated to serve U.S. foreign policy and national security interests, not the interests of the poor countries. There was, moreover, no evidence that the U.S. electorate supported the idealists' view. Rather, the voters' concern about the diversion of resources from domestic needs to aid forced the Congress to justify expenditures for foreign economic aid in terms of its benefits for U.S. national security.

Objectives of Other Donors

The national security purposes of U.S. economic aid, which in the early 1950s were primarily to buttress resistance to Communist military or subversive aggression, gradually expanded to include rewarding friends and punishing enemies; gaining influence over the foreign policy orientation of Third World governments; retaining that influence once achieved; and precluding Communist donors from attaining a foreign policy success. Aid in fact became the major weapon of the United States in the cold war as it was waged in the Third World.

That choice of weapon was confirmed by the Soviet Union. In 1954, Chairman Nikita Khrushchev announced that developing countries attempting to raise living standards no longer "need go begging to their former oppressors"; they could get modern equipment from socialist countries with no strings attached.[23] How concessionary the terms of Soviet (including the Council for Mutual Economic Assistance [CMEA]) foreign aid were has been disputed for years; the poor quality of Soviet products meant that they could be exported only at cut-rate prices. For our purposes the issue is not important; the Communists early on had developed considerable skill at killing two birds with one stone. Their aid program appeared to be aimed both at marketing exports and gaining influence.

It succeeded in both. In addition, after its initiation the "Communist Economic Offensive in Developing Countries" (as it was called in the title of a joint CIA/State Department/USAID classified biweekly publication reporting on the subject that appeared in the second half of the 1950s) energized the U.S. aid program. Mosley characterized the 1950s as the decade when the "market for aid transfers" shifted from virtual U.S. monopoly during the first half to U.S.-Soviet duopoly in the second half.[24]

During the 1950s, the U.S. aid program was administered through a variety of programs, organizations, and mandates; it was not until 1961 that the first unified development assistance legislation was enacted. Before 1961, U.S. defense and military aid were administered separately under the Mutual Security Program managed by the Defense Department, although from 1951 to 1953 the Mutual Security Agency was responsible for both economic and military aid.[25] Economic aid was handled by a variety of agencies, including the military during the 1940s and the Foreign Operations Administration and Economic Cooperation Administration in the 1950s.

The landmark Foreign Assistance Act of 1961 stated the purposes of the legislation thus:

> An Act to promote the foreign policy, security and general welfare of the United States by assisting peoples of the world in their efforts toward economic development and internal and external security, and for other purposes.

This act, which has been amended regularly since 1961, is still the basic foreign aid mandate of the United States.

In the three decades since the act was passed, the specific goals of the program have mushroomed; they have nonetheless continuously affirmed that the "individual liberties, economic prosperity and security of the people of the United States" will be enhanced by a program of aid for foreign economic development. The recent words of Richard Bissell, one of the top administrators of the U.S. aid program, summarize concisely the complexities introduced into the aid program during the three decades. Bissell wrote in *The Washington Quarterly* that

> With the multiplication of assistance purposes over a 30-year period, the program has inevitably generated internal contradictions. The uneasiness of the relationship between

economic and security goals has intensified with the
changing role of the United States in the world of the 1980s
and 1990s. The generosity associated with development
assistance has come under attack from those concerned
about export promotion. The support lent to friendly
regimes through military assistance can easily run counter
to the human rights goals of the administration. At the
same time, the government's ability to even out these
contradictions has inevitably diminished. As the group of
players has expanded over the last 10 years, coordination
has become progressively more difficult, and the Gramm-
Rudman pressures have only exacerbated the situation.[26]

The case studies illustrate the complexities Bissell spells out.

Enthusiasm for foreign aid, which had never achieved great
heights of popularity in the United States, began to be undermined during the 1960s. The Congress and the public grew
restive when a series of military coups in Latin American
countries that were experiencing rapid economic growth
replaced democratic regimes with military dictators. Economic
development, apparently, was not sufficient for political stability and democracy. Aid began to develop a credibility problem
in some circles.

The problem was exacerbated by the fact that academia,
which had enthusiastically embraced the concept of foreign
aid, had uncritically accepted the prevailing consensus that
economic development was essential for political stability. A
growing collection of cases indicated that economic development, if necessary, was not sufficient to support existing
democratic regimes, thus undermining at least the most sim-
plistic version of the rationale for economic aid adduced by all
postwar administrations.

Aid's credibility problem was further aggravated as the
1960s moved on by accumulating evidence that economic
growth did not necessarily benefit the poorest groups in the
recipient countries. Economic improvement did not "trickle
down." Evidence also began to accumulate that there was a
limit to the absorptive capacity of the developing countries
that restricted their abilities to spend aid funds, a limit that
had not been anticipated. (The main reason for a low level of

economic development had been assumed to be lack of capital.) Increasingly it became clear that the process of economic development and its relationship to political development were far more complex than they were originally understood to be.[27]

During the 1960s the virtual aid duopoly of the USSR and the United States was broken as other donor countries began programs of support for economic development in the developing world. At the same time the role of the World Bank and other multilateral aid agencies was also expanding, with a larger share of U.S. economic aid being channeled through them.[28] As a consequence, World Bank aid, which in 1960 amounted to one-quarter of that of the United States, by 1988 was four times that of the United States.[29] Similarly, the U.S. share of global Official Development Assistance (ODA) declined from 57 percent in 1960 to 37 percent in 1970 and 16 percent today.[30] (In the 1980s two former aid recipients, Taiwan and Korea, joined the list of donor countries—certainly a sign that the aid program did something well). Because ODA is defined to omit military aid (for the most part) it understates the share of the United States; nonetheless the trend is dramatic.[31]

The data in the case studies on total foreign aid received by each country from individual donors are not comparable, relating as they do to different time periods and with differences in coverage. The data do indicate, however, a much smaller U.S. share than is generally assumed by the Congress or the public. The share of the United States in total ODA received by Korea through 1984 was less than one-third;[32] for Pakistan for the 1980s the U.S. share was 17 percent;[33] for the Philippines for the year 1989–1990 it was less than 5 percent (although including base support in the U.S. aid raises its share to 23 percent).[34] Mexico received no bilateral or multilateral aid during the 1980s, although it did accept small amounts of food, family planning, and narcotics assistance.[35] In most cases the World Bank or Japan was the largest single donor.

To a large degree the motivations underlying the aid programs of the new donors were economic and commercial. Colonies did not become self-supporting with the raising of their own flag; as former colonies became independent, bud-

getary grants from the metropole took the form of economic
aid to now sovereign governments. In addition the metropole
undertook to retain and even expand existing commercial ties
by grants and loans for developmental purposes that were
required to be spent in the donor country. At the same time
national security considerations probably played some role in
the economic aid programs of former colonial powers: the
desire to maintain a bloc of international support for their
foreign policy objectives. Apart from those of the former
colonial powers, the underlying motivations of new economic
aid programs appear to have been primarily economic and
humanitarian. The World Bank, of course, was prohibited by
its charter from political considerations in granting credits and
loans (a prohibition not always observed).[36]

As the aid programs of other donors matured through the
1970s and 1980s, they became increasingly commercial and
competitive in motivation. This trend reflected the more
intensely competitive international markets of the last years of
the century and the concomitant attempts of governments to
promote their own exports. It was a period during which the
United States became increasingly isolated in its support for
open competitive world markets. Aid donor agencies in Europe
and Japan used aid funds to support their own exporters
through tied aid and other more sophisticated techniques. The
United States, meanwhile, continued to be willing to sacrifice
its commercial interests to foreign policy requirements.[37]

The primacy given by the United States to national security goals in its economic aid program thus appears to be
unique. Even the USSR appears to have placed more weight on
the aim of developing a market for its exports than did the
United States. Certainly Japan and most of Europe did.

The multiplication of donor countries and institutions
meant that the influence of each donor on the recipient was
weakened. In addition, the fact that other donor countries
used aid to further their own commercial interests while the
United States sacrificed its commercial well-being in the face
of mounting balance of payments problems also led earlier aid
supporters in the United States to question the usefulness of
the aid program. Aid fatigue mounted.

Chapter II
Foreign Economic Aid as an Instrument of National Security Policy: Cases and the Overall Record

In the 45 years after World War II, all U.S. foreign assistance programs were shaped by the overriding objective of prevailing in the strategic rivalry with the Soviet Union. Within this context, the United States viewed its national security interests in terms of peace and freedom around the world. Peace entailed political stability within and between countries; freedom entailed democracy or at least democratization. Dr. Thunberg's reading of the historical record shows that for the first decade and a half, political stability was believed to rest on economic growth, but when several rapidly growing developing countries experienced military coups, it became evident that economic growth, if a necessary condition, was not a sufficient condition for political stability. It also became clear that the relationship between economic development, democracy, and political stability was far more complex than had been originally assumed, and thus that the relation between U.S. national security and economic development in the developing world was not well understood. It still is not.

Aid legislation itself does not usually specify which goal has top priority, except implicitly in the order in which the objectives are mentioned. Even accepting order as an indication of priority, the legislation is still silent on the subject of time span. The evidence of the case studies is that the short run was usually given priority over the long run. The case studies, and the informal review of the postwar record by the regional studies sections of CSIS, also reveal a fairly consistent pattern in which the national security goal is given priority over other goals.

An evaluation of one part of a multigoal aid program is complicated by the fact that the difference between gross and net accomplishments is likely to be large and to vary considerably from case to case, by the distance that may exist between cause and eventual effect, by the fact that one event's following another does not indicate cause and effect, and by the presence, always, of significant unintended consequences. Finally, evaluation of a foreign aid program is blurred by the fact that aid is only one facet of the totality of bilateral relations existing between the donor and recipient countries. Trade in goods and services, investment by the private sector, tourism, and diplomacy (traditional and public) all provide a network of ongoing contacts that influence the success of any single U.S. policy initiative.

Still it is possible to identify, separate, and assess some of the effects of economic assistance programs in furthering the noneconomic objectives of the United States during this period. Identifying these effects leads to important insights about the ways in which economic aid can contribute to objectives other than economic performance.

The case studies reveal the limitations of economic assistance as a policy instrument for achieving noneconomic objectives. But, as previewed at the beginning of this report, they also reveal conditions determining the probability of success or failure.

In the next chapter, consideration is given to the relationship between the purposes aid was designed to serve during the cold war and purposes it may serve in the future. In the cases of South Korea, the Philippines, and Pakistan, economic assistance complemented security assistance in serving major U.S. security interests, and the mixed economic results were not necessarily a major concern at the time. Earlier, we cited Delal Baer's indication that cold war concerns were not absent from Washington's thinking about how to help Mexico either.

Because the study is designed to assist policymakers in their consideration of *future* programs, and because "traditional" official economic assistance may be a diminishing part of the mix, the study's net has been cast wider to include other forms of assistance that still involve the transfer of economic resources, in some fashion, in a way favorable to the recipient country. This is the particular point of the inclusion of Mexico as a case study, along with other forms of assistance given to the other case-study countries.

Economic aid has been employed both as a direct and an indirect instrument of national security policy. In its *direct* form, aid has been used essentially as a bribe or a threat (although couched in terms of cooperation for shared security objectives—at least until the Philippines started insisting on calling rent by its proper name). The clear, if not always clearly stated, purpose was to gain influence over the foreign policy orientation of a government: to reward friends, or to punish nonsupporters by withholding aid, and to preclude Communist donors from achieving a success. As such it has typically aimed at a short-term, fairly immediate target. In contrast, the *indirect* use of aid as a security instrument addressed a mix of presumably interrelated long-term objectives: ensuring U.S. national security, political stability, and democratization in the future as rising standards of living and an expanding middle class in the developing country endow it with greater freedom of choice in both the political and economic realms.

Here the difficulties begin even before one examines the relation between the aid and political change. We know, now, that democratization frequently produces the emergence, and at least temporary political success, of radicalism. That radicalism, although it may be a genuine reflection of the will of the people at the moment, is often directly at odds with some of the other aid objectives, especially stability and friendliness toward the United States. Another common conflict between objectives is becoming more clear with each passing day in the newly industrializing countries (NICs) of Southeast Asia: the development of a middle class, though often seen in the West as a formula for stability and moderation, can be, in other political cultures, a political powder keg. A modernizing middle class appears frequently to reach a point where it becomes conscious of the incompatibility of its own modern, material goals and the country's traditional politics. The result is often a rebellion made by the middle class, as in Thailand. (The surprise shown by some Westerners, journalists, and the now-endangered old regime reveals an inadequate study of, for example, the stages of the French Revolution.) But the postwar assumption was that as support for democracy and free enterprise spread around the world, U.S. national security would be strengthened.

There have been innumerable opportunities to test how successfully economic aid can be used directly as a bribe or threat in the short run. Testing the success of the indirect use of aid even in the gross sense is more ambiguous because the definition of "long run" is essentially open ended. This leads us to the concentric circles of causation outlined in the opening section of this report. That X immediately follows Y does not mean that Y was the cause of X. That X appears years later does not mean that Y was not at least a crucial *part* of the cause. Closer analysis is required to make the distinctions, especially in a case such as Korea, where some of the stated objectives of the aid did in fact come about, but where the causal relationship is dubious. If it appears that economic aid has not been successful as an indirect means toward heightened U.S. national security in a particular case, it may be that not enough time has been allowed. The opposite may also be true: too early an assessment may yield a false *positive*. This underscores the virtue of the Korean case, where the time frame is extensive.

The record of economic aid as an instrument of national security policy revealed by the case studies is mixed. There have been *apparent* successes and failures with both direct and indirect uses. Each of the case studies notes a basic conflict between short-term and long-term U.S. goals. The incompatibility of U.S. support for democratization—a long-term goal in countries like Korea, Pakistan, and the Philippines with authoritarian regimes and little or no history of democracy—and the U.S. search for short-run political stability in the face of an immediate external or internal threat appears in each case study. The United States has supported an authoritarian regime (or successive oppressive regimes) in each case, not being willing to risk political instability by pushing for a change. In the case of Korea the immediate threat was an invasion from the North;[1] in Pakistan it was the Soviet aggression in Afghanistan;[2] in the Philippines it was the Communist insurgency[3] and then later opposition to Aquino.[4] In each case support for progress on human rights, individual freedoms, and democracy was sacrificed for immediate political stability. (In the last case, however, it was long-term political stability in the Philippines that may have been sacrificed—by the failure to pursue economic reforms—in order to protect the immediate democratic gains of the Aquino presidency.)

Mexico

The case of Mexico is distinct. It is, of course, useless for any conclusions about official economic assistance. Nevertheless, by the very fact that Washington used a different repertoire of tools, most of them *not* unique to Mexico, the scope of the lessons learned from this study is thus expanded to include programs that may frequently be on policymakers' tables in the future. Its political, social, and security objectives, in large measure different from those in the other cases, loom large for the future. The noneconomic objectives of U.S. economic policy toward Mexico include: (1) deterrence of hostile third-country intervention; (2) prevention of political instability and violent disorder; (3) diminution rather than growth in illegal immigration to the United States; (4) prevention of growth in illegal narcotics trafficking to the pervasive level reached in Colombia; and (5) promotion of stable democracy. It is hoped, for example, that when the North America Free Trade Agreement (NAFTA) comes into being, economic growth in Mexico will reduce the illegal inflows of immigrants and narcotics to the United States. U.S. tariff reduction is the chosen national security instrument in the case of Mexico. At some indeterminate time in the future, however, we may see Mexico as a primary case study of the indirect long-term use of aid for national security purposes of the post–cold war variety.

In the 1980s the relative political stability and economic success of Mexico over the preceding 60 years was disrupted by the threat of economic collapse and radical political change. The greatest immediate danger to the United States came from the possibility of a precipitous worsening of illegal immigration and narcotics trafficking, already serious problems. The crisis produced unprecedented economic collaboration between the two countries, aimed at restructuring the Mexican economy and laying the foundation for progressive political change.

Mexico poses a unique challenge to economic policy. With its fierce nationalism and fear of increased U.S. leverage in its domestic affairs, it has largely rejected U.S. development assistance. In these circumstances the United States has had little to offer beyond its markets, its support in multilateral institutions, and its expertise and commitment to market economics. The United States has pursued a "Mexico first" pattern of economic relations, supporting Mexican access to the Generalized System of Preference (GSP) in 1975 and special treatment under items 806.30 and 807.00 of the U.S. Tariff Schedule. The United States helped to stave off a Mexican loan default in 1982 with a Treasury bridge loan and advanced cash to Mexico for the purchase of oil for the U.S. petroleum reserve. Although announced early in 1989 in response to violence in Venezuela, the Brady plan for debt rescheduling was first applied to Mexico.

The combination of Mexican pride and U.S. penury has produced a cutting-edge approach to economic policy based on economic restructuring and trade integration. This policy evolved throughout the 1980s, stimulated by President Ronald Reagan's use of the bully pulpit to spread the gospel of market economics and his bold support for NAFTA. It reached its most complete expression in the announced intention of U.S. president George Bush and Mexican president Carlos Salinas de Gortari to enter into such an agreement.

The "Mexico first" approach is evident in President Bush's Enterprise for the Americas initiative. The concept of this initiative is to reward nations that have implemented sound economic policies by providing free trade with the United States, reduction in official U.S. concessionary debt, and access to a $300 million multilateral development fund. Countries such as Mexico and Chile, which have advanced farthest down the path of investment and trade liberalization, are the benchmark performers and have set the standard for other Latin American nations.

The ultimate political success of this economic policy rests on a largely untested hypothesis. The concept is that a successful, functioning market economy operating in conjunction with the United States will discredit the policy prescriptions advocated by the Mexican Left and lead to broad acceptance of foreign investment combined with privatization of state-owned enterprises. The development of political consensus on economic policy would have a profound impact on the parameters of political debate in Mexico and, ultimately, on its prospects for stable democracy.

Economic success in Chile generated such a consensus and led the Christian Democrat-to-socialist coalition succeeding Augusto Pinochet Ugarte to sustain his economic reforms, which had curbed inflation and brought consistent growth. Consensus on economic policy has moderated the extreme Left and undercut the scare tactics of the far Right. Economic consensus may be an important precondition to stable multiparty democracy elsewhere in Latin America. In Chile consensus regarding economic policy made possible a smooth transition to democracy and the election of a coalition including moderate socialists. It remains to be seen whether the Chilean experience can be repeated in Mexico and other Latin American countries.

The case of Mexico reveals other aspects of the linkage between economic and political reform. Before Mexico began the reform process in 1982, it was a strong centralized state buttressed by an aging but still effective dominant single party. Mass political participation was controlled and coopted through an extensive range of corporatist social and political organizations linked to the dominant party. Social conflicts were eased by patronage and ideological flexibility. The modus operandi of the regime was traditional patron-client relations with a thin veneer of modern, distributionist rhetoric.

The unleashing of market forces undermines authoritarian rule and foments the evolution of a more pluralistic, liberal democratic environment. Market-based economies decrease, by definition, the leverage and power of the state. Privatization decreases the patronage available for political allies. The removal of import licensing decreases government leverage over the entrepreneurial elites. Deregulation decentralizes decision making and increases regional autonomy. Paring back federal deficits and relying on the market to set prices and wages interferes with granting subsidies to favored constituencies. Paradoxically, all these policies require a strong state to implement them, but they simultaneously undercut the traditional power and strength of a centralized regime like the Mexican Institutional Revolutionary Party (PRI).

According to this line of reasoning, economic liberalism leads to political liberalism, but not necessarily in a linear fashion. Initially, economic reform may be destabilizing and so difficult politically that only a strong or even authoritarian government is capable of withstanding the years of pain before reform begins to pay off and generate significant supporting constituencies. The economic pain resulting from Mexican economic reform efforts initially caused political support for the PRI to plummet. Although this trend has been reversed, the ultimate outcome is far from decided. The most successful cases of economic reform to date have occurred in authoritarian environments—Chile, South Korea, Taiwan, and Singapore.

Preferential tariff treatment for Mexico is appropriately considered aid because it is a transfer of resources on concessionary terms. Without the concession, the higher tariffs that would have been paid on imports from Mexico would have been borne in part by Mexican producers and workers (in the form of lower incomes), in part by the U.S. consumers (in higher prices). The cost to the U.S. government and thus the U.S. taxpayer would lie in the tariff revenue lost by the concession, although if demand were sufficiently elastic, the government might collect more revenue at the lower than at the higher duty.

The United States has invested heavily in the future of economic reform in Mexico. It has done so in hopes of stabilizing its southern neighbor and countering the threats of massive illegal immigration and narcotics trafficking. As author Delal Baer observes, however, the U.S. government appears not to have thought out systematically the relationship between the strategy of supporting economic change and the achievement of its noneconomic objectives. Rather than an orderly straight-line process, economic, social, and political progress is likely to be fraught with conflict and instability. The art of policy is managing the political fallout of transition. In this realm economic policy has proved to be a blunt instrument.[5]

Baer's concluding analysis probes further into the relationship between economic progress and political liberalization:

The process of economic reform in the short run seems to weaken stability and stimulate authoritarian responses. Economic reformers may be unwilling to sacrifice their reforms to the vagaries of democracy. In the mid to long term, the same forces that lead to authoritarian rule may also lead to democratization of authoritarian regimes. Thus, in successful economic reforms such as those of Chile and South Korea, the undermining of authoritarian institutions by market forces might ultimately contribute to a reopening of the political system. Most fundamentally, the basing of an economy on individual initiative may undermine authoritarian civic culture. However, the successful, irreversible implementation of the economic reform model may be a precondition to successful political reform.[6]

Because the Mexican case study is the only one of the four that is primarily forward-looking rather than historical in treatment, it offers little present scope for testing. The study nonetheless is rich in its analyses of the relationships among the variables important in this effort. It notes a theme running throughout the case studies: the conflict between short-term and long-term U.S. goals. It points out that the United States must choose between progress toward democratization in Mexico in the short run, with its heightened potential for a failure in immigration and drug goals in the long term (as a consequence of political instability stemming from too-rapid democratization), or a more probable long-run success for its immigration and drug policy with a postponement of democratization in the near term.[7]

Dr. Baer also points out that economic growth, while likely to diminish immigration in the long run, is unlikely in the short run to generate enough new jobs to absorb the awesome number of new entrants to the labor force every year.[8] Whether U.S. policy will be sufficiently patient to await the potential long-run benefits of significant declines in immigration from Mexico remains to be seen.

The debt relief that the United States provided to Mexico in the 1980s—again a concessionary transfer of resources, but still an unorthodox form of aid—is of ambiguous effectiveness. Without the emergency aid provided by the U.S. government in 1982, unemployment and the decline in real incomes in Mexico might have been much worse than actually occurred and the movement of immigrants and drugs much heavier. Such a conclusion, however, is a worst-case scenario, not necessarily the most probable. In any event, the object of this aid was the stability of the U.S. and international banking systems, not economic activity in Mexico. The objective of financial stability was met, with the possibility of some positive side effects on other U.S. national security objectives.

Although much of the case study of Mexico is analytical and speculative, it is the most forward-looking of the four case studies and, as such, provides the most intriguing insights respecting the possible future relationship between economic assistance and the noneconomic objectives of the United States.

Korea

Economic assistance to Korea started in 1945 immediately upon the withdrawal of the defeated Japanese; it was viewed as short-term emergency aid to prevent starvation and disease. The U.S. Army fed the Koreans and undertook to revive agriculture and industry. While official Washington vacillated over Korean policy, aid continued at a declining level until the 1950 invasion from the North and the beginning of the resistance backed by the United Nations (UN).[9] The level of U.S. aid jumped during the war and despite many problems with the Korean strongman, Syngman Rhee, the United States undertook a long-term aid commitment to the country at the war's end in 1953. Between 1953 and 1969 over $3 billion flowed from the United States to Korea.

So the goals of U.S. aid moved through the stages of rescuing the Korean economy, then keeping the economy from collapsing under the burden of the Korean War, and finally supporting the buildup of defense capabilities against the threat of renewed aggression from the north.

The military and economic goals were intertwined. To make Korea militarily self-supporting, its economy had to be first rebuilt and then developed. Rhee, however, refused to agree to an armistice with the North and was a constant source of trouble for the United States. Mazarr notes that his administration was "an unending parade of corruption and inefficiency" that at least contributed to, perhaps accounted for, the high cost and inefficiencies in administering the U.S. aid program.[10] Aid was used both as a carrot and a stick in attempting to induce Rhee to abandon his plans for retaking the North and to agree to the armistice but to no avail.[11] Rhee also embarrassed the United States by his repeated offenses against human rights. The United States put up with Rhee and with Park Chung Hee, who succeeded him in a military coup (after a brief interlude of democracy), as part of its immediate cold war efforts to resist Communist gains, despite the cost in individual freedoms in Korea and in progress toward a long-term goal of democracy.

The problem was not all on the Korean side. Once the two basic aims of military self-sufficiency and economic relief were achieved, U.S. officials often expressed confusion about whether their primary task was to promote economic efficiency or democratization or social stability. Many goals competed for attention and resources, with the result that all were diluted. In part this represented a misapplication of lessons from the Marshall Plan, whose success suggested that economic assistance would promote a host of noneconomic goals. In fact, the European case was nearly unique; it involved the postwar rehabilitation of advanced industrial democracies, not the construction of a developing-world economy from scratch. With such a poor definition of goals, it is no surprise that none were well served.

The program may have been successful in fulfilling its initial economic goals, but that success did not extend to the next level, the expected political consequences: despite the U.S. belief that the aid program could foster democracy, authoritarian government continued.

Particularly during the years when Syngman Rhee was in power, the U.S. aid program afforded Washington very limited leverage with Seoul because withholding aid would have jeopardized objectives that were nearly as important to the United States as they were to South Korea. Only after Park Chung Hee seized power in 1961 did the potential for withdrawal of U.S. support have any significant impact, and then it helped to precipitate a highly significant turning point. For some time after the coup the United States openly condemned the action and showed distrust for the undemocratic Park regime. Formal relations became even more strained than they had been during Syngman Rhee's administration. Fearing that long-term U.S. support was no longer guaranteed, Park and his compatriots decided on a course of action aimed at much greater economic and military independence from the United States. In the end this decision led to the "economic miracle" that propelled South Korea into the top rank of newly industrialized countries. Thus was the ultimate aim of all U.S. aid programs—self-sufficiency and the end of aid—realized in South Korea.

There is general agreement that U.S. aid laid the foundation for the Korean economic miracle, but this is not to say that aid guarantees growth. South Korea possessed essential ingredients that are not always present: a national leader committed to economic progress; a competent government economic team; effective communications between the government and the people; and an educated, industrious work force. Without these ingredients, especially the driving leadership of Park, South Korea would not have been such a shining example of the fruits of foreign aid and investment.

During the 40 years of U.S. grant assistance to South Korea there was no lasting progress toward functioning democracy, despite U.S. efforts to bring this about. One authoritarian ruler after another held power. It is not necessarily a paradox that the transition to democracy gained momentum after the country was no longer dependent on U.S. aid. Many factors contributed to the elections of 1987 won by Roh Tae Woo, but one certainly has to be the economic progress that had been achieved and opened the way for the people to act on their aspirations.

The Korean study highlights several lessons, six of which have general importance for the overall study:

- Economic aid is a blunt, not subtle, tool.
- Aid is a very long-term proposition. (When the other cases are also taken into account, this statement must be modified to say that aid is *usually* a long-term proposition, although there are some very instructive short-term instances, as in the Philippines.)
- Aid should be focused on public, rather than government, support. (Here the study calls attention to the potential importance of public diplomacy, saying that "in many instances the cultivation of public support . . . can contribute more to U.S. interests in the long term than support for a specific regime."[12])
- The objectives of aid programs should be clearly defined, few in number, and general in character.
- Aid does not confer a significant ability to force reforms in the recipient country. (This would certainly be an impression any observer would derive from the Korean case. When it is mixed with the other cases, however, the conclusion is that there are factors that make it more or less possible to force reforms.)
- Although not granting immediate leverage, aid can—and should—be targeted by the donor.

The Korean study, like the others, is also rich in meaning for the accomplishment of *economic* goals through assistance programs. See, for example, the two "lessons" in the study, which highlight the importance of human resource development and the fact that successful aid can create an economic competitor for the donor.[13] But for the focus of the overall study, the conclusions of the analyst responsible for the Korean study illustrate the value of multiple cases, as opposed to the biopsy approach: mixing the Korea findings with those of the other case studies produces some indications that are quite different from any that might stem from the single study standing alone.

The Philippines

The United States has been closely involved with the Philippines for twice as long as with Korea but without the same happy outcome. The case study focuses on the years 1979 to 1991.[14] During this period U.S. economic assistance to the Philippines supported three noneconomic objectives: (1) maintenance of base rights; (2) containment of the Communist insurgency; and (3) progress toward democracy and respect for human rights—with the base rights objective paramount. As long as the bases were the source of patronage funds that kept Marcos in power, he and the United States could agree on the first two objectives. The advent of the Aquino regime, which did provide progress on the third goal, probably would have caused the first to be abandoned even if Mount Pinatubo had not accelerated matters. Meanwhile, however, the shift in the international posture of the USSR meant not so great a perceived loss for U.S. national security as would have been the case a year or two earlier.

Until 1979 cooperation with the Philippines followed the traditional cold war paradigm. U.S. forward deployments were intended as much for the security of the host country as for the protection of U.S. interests. U.S. aid was given not as compensation for base rights but to bolster the host country's ability to share in its own defense. By improving the living conditions of the people, economic aid would counter the appeal of Communist propaganda and increase the commitment to remain allied with the West.

In 1979 the Philippine government abandoned all pretense of accepting this formulation and openly demanded "rent," which, presumably, it could use for its own political purposes. Thus, each side had other objectives that tended to dilute its commitment to the economic purposes of the aid program. Nevertheless, economic aid to the Philippines was implemented by USAID with an elaborate set of development objectives and projects.

Although U.S. economic assistance provided the requisite quid pro quo, the linkage to U.S. base rights had serious adverse consequences for the noneconomic objectives it was supposed to support. Confusion over the level of aid to be provided under the "best efforts" pledge weakened the U.S. position in subsequent base negotiations. Throughout the Philippines the United States came to be viewed as supporting

the Marcos regime primarily to keep the bases. This perception
was exploited by supporters of the Communist insurgency.
The Marcos family disbursed much of the aid as political
patronage, thwarting rather than furthering democratic reform.

The results from the economic aid program fell far short of
its objectives, especially in the case of the Rural Development
Fund (RDF) for the construction of schools and other social
infrastructure. U.S. budget support provided on the condition
that the Philippine government reform the economy was
largely ineffective; the conditions lacked credibility in light of
the noneconomic objectives involved. Then, when Corazon
Aquino became president, the aid given to show political
support was so generous in relation to immediate needs that it
undermined the incentive for economic reform. Preoccupation
with noneconomic objectives distorted the economic assistance program and prevented support for sectors, such as
telecommunications and electric power generation, that would
have been more beneficial to both U.S. exports and investment
in the Philippines than the programs undertaken.

In his assessment of these problems Ernest Preeg empha-
sizes the need for aid programs carefully designed to provide
economic results that will be advantageous to both the donor
and the recipient over the longer term, taking into account the
strengths and limitations of each side. If the limited U.S.
economic aid to the Philippines continues to be perceived by
both sides as linked to U.S. security interests, U.S. trade and
investment will continue to lose ground to other donors,
particularly Japan.

In sum, U.S. base support and support for fighting the
insurgency in the Philippines contributed to corruption and
economic mismanagement in the Marcos regime and, in
delaying economic reform, it actually furthered long-term
political instability. U.S. base rights were retained, but they
were the source of mounting bilateral misunderstanding and,
within the Philippines, of a spreading resentment over the fact
that the United States was willing to keep Marcos in power in
order to retain its bases. The difficulties suffered by the U.S.
effort to support the Aquino regime are a virtual catalog of the
negative side of the lessons learned from the four case studies
and the additional research.

The price for our ignoring (or ignorance of) those norms is still being paid. The Philippines continues to experience erratic growth and political instability while postponing badly needed economic reforms. It is true, of course, that the advent of Aquino's "people power," the holding of elections, and the probable successful transfer of power this year are all in line with the U.S. stress on democratic values in the rhetoric surrounding our aid program. But we can take only qualified comfort from the route traveled and the real relationship between U.S. programs and democratization.

Pakistan

In the cases of Korea and the Philippines, the high level of U.S. security interest attached to economic aid gave leverage to the aid recipient rather than the donor. The same point is illustrated in the case of Pakistan. Pakistan had almost total control over the distribution of aid—from the United States and elsewhere—to the Afghan resistance, channeling it to the groups least acceptable from the U.S. perspective.[15] Also, before the withdrawal of Soviet forces, a U.S. threat to cut off aid over human rights abuses or nuclear proliferation was lacking in credibility.[16]

Even after the withdrawal of Soviet forces from Afghanistan, when the cutoff threat became credible and U.S. aid actually ceased, nuclear capability was very probably more important to Pakistan than U.S. economic aid, especially in view of the inconstancy in the history of the U.S. aid program in Pakistan.[17] Pakistan perceived its main national security threat not from the USSR but from India, which had already achieved a nuclear capability.

U.S. aid to Pakistan began in the early 1950s shortly after the creation of the state of Pakistan. From the beginning cold war considerations dominated the provision of aid, and economic assistance complemented military assistance.

During the Afghan war, for example, the bulk of U.S. economic assistance came from the Economic Support Fund, was spent on essential imports, and served to offset the cost of Pakistan's purchases of U.S. military equipment. It is useful to note that the Reagan administration would probably have been

quite willing to grant Pakistan the military aid to cover the
cost of its two squadrons of 40 F-16 fighter aircraft, but the
majority in Congress would not have voted such a large military grant to a country such as Pakistan. The way around this
legislative problem was to enact credits for the military sale
and grant economic aid to offset the burden on Pakistan's
economy. This solution helped to maintain the annual balance
between military and economic aid funds that has long preoc-
cupied concerned members of Congress.

Because it has been driven primarily by cold war considerations, the U.S. interest in Pakistan has fluctuated with the ebb
and flow of the U.S.-Soviet rivalry. At times, however, other
subsidiary interests have helped enhance this basic U.S.
interest in Pakistan. In the late 1960s and the early 1970s, for
example, the United States was interested in using Pakistan as
a channel of communication with the People's Republic of
China (PRC), with which Pakistan had excellent relations.
Similarly, in the 1980s, because of the break with Iran following the Islamic revolution there, the United States became
more interested in Pakistan as a factor in its strategy for the
security of the Persian Gulf. This further enhancement of the
strategic importance of Pakistan came at a time when U.S.
interest had already reached an all-time high because of the
Soviet invasion of Afghanistan. Pakistan was the main frontline
state in the fight against the Soviet presence.

From Pakistan's perspective, however, only during certain
periods, such as the 1980s, has the Soviet threat been the
main reason for cooperation with the United States. For longer
periods, other security concerns, particularly its conflict with
India, have been the more important reasons for Pakistan's
seeking U.S. cooperation.

This basic asymmetry in U.S.-Pakistan interests has resulted in an unstable alliance, which has alternated between
periods of close cooperation—as in the 1950s and 1980s—and
conditions of near hostility—as in the mid to late 1970s.

The level of security and economic assistance to Pakistan
has fluctuated as a function of the perceived importance of
Pakistan in the pursuit of U.S. political and strategic goals. U.S.
economic assistance reached its peak in the 1980s as Pakistan

acquired a pivotal role in U.S. efforts to roll back Soviet advances in Afghanistan. The freeze on U.S. aid to Pakistan since October 1990 reflects the new regional realities, most notably the withdrawal of Soviet troops from Afghanistan, which dramatically reduced Pakistan's strategic significance to the United States.

The character of U.S. aid to Pakistan, as well as the effectiveness of the aid in achieving local economic, social, and political goals, has also been affected by the level of U.S. strategic interest in that country. At times when the United States has had an overriding strategic interest in Pakistan, as during the 1980s, it has not been able to use economic assistance to achieve other goals. Throughout the 1980s, for example, the United States had only limited success in using economic assistance to help fight drug trafficking, encourage democracy, forestall nuclear proliferation, and promote economic reform. When the cooperation of a recipient is vitally important to a donor, the recipient enjoys added leverage with the donor and is able to resist donor pressure to pursue secondary goals.

The history of the U.S.-Pakistan aid relationship offered in the study is validation of the view, long prevalent in the development community, that economic assistance motivated by security and political interests is of limited value as an agent of economic development and social and political reform.

Consistent with this view, there has been recurring tension between short-term U.S. goals in Pakistan—to keep it in the Western camp and secure its cooperation in the containment of Soviet expansionism—and the long-term U.S. interest in helping Pakistan develop a self-sufficient economy, democratic government, and more equitable social conditions.

Although economic assistance has contributed to achieving U.S. strategic goals, it has not been the most important factor. U.S. military assistance and the U.S. security umbrella have been more important than economic aid in securing Pakistan's cooperation in advancing U.S. strategic interests. There were periods, as in the example of the Afghan war cited earlier, when the primary function of U.S. economic assistance was to offset the cost of Pakistan's purchases of U.S. military equipment.

Throughout the history recounted in the case study (but especially during the years before the Soviet invasion of Afghanistan, from 1951 to 1979), the impact of U.S. assistance in prompting Pakistani cooperation depended on the extent to which Pakistan shared U.S. goals. Dr. Shireen Hunter observes that if Pakistan "accepted American funds but not the validity of underlying U.S. initiatives, progress on the issues in question was negligible."[18]

Individual freedoms were not the only sacrifice. Dr. Hunter notes that U.S. support for the Afghan rebels through Pakistan helped to create a local mafia and the "culture of heroin-Kalashnikov."[19] And it exacerbated ethnic and sectarian problems, overmilitarization, and the erosion of law and order.[20]

As was the case in the Philippines, in Pakistan also the price is still being paid. Although it may be that in Pakistan knowledge of the strong U.S. attitude favoring democracy contributed to a limited process of democratization in various periods, including the present, it is also true that Pakistan continues to experience erratic growth and political instability while postponing badly needed economic reforms.

Sub-Saharan Africa

A separate CSIS two-year study under the sponsorship of USAID employed case studies of five countries—*The Gambia, Ghana, Kenya, Mali,* and *Zambia*—to investigate the ways in which politics influences the success of economic reform programs undertaken in conjunction with economic assistance from international financial institutions and bilateral donors. The findings of this study reflect primarily conditions in Africa, but some have wider application and are relevant to the issue of employing economic aid to achieve noneconomic objectives in the Third World. Here is a selection of those findings:

• There have been dramatic changes in a number of African countries in 1990 and 1991. These changes resulted primarily from massive public discontent over the continuing economic failure of African governments. Discontent over economic conditions led to demands for political change. And change in one country increased the pressure for change in neighboring states.

- Whereas the primary impetus for economic reform has come from donors, the driving force for political change appears to be internal, not external.
- Experience in countries such as the Gambia indicates that a democratic government does not necessarily guarantee good governance. Transparency and accountability may exist in theory, but they will not secure good governance unless the citizenry is active politically and calls elected officials to account.
- Many inside and outside of Africa perceive democracy and development as being linked, the one likely to promote the other. Reality may be more complex and less reassuring.
- The evidence from sub-Saharan Africa and developing countries of other regions indicates that good governance is necessary for economic growth to occur, but not that democracy guarantees good governance or that autocratic rule precludes it.
- Given the present state of political development in most states of sub-Saharan Africa, it is not clear that political liberalization will necessarily put the governments there in a stronger position to exercise the kind of economic discipline that has characterized cases of sustained economic development throughout the world since 1945.
- Many of the new governments in sub-Saharan Africa owe their rise to power to constituencies that are the beneficiaries of current policies and practices inimical to economic growth. These governments face the dilemma that they may be able to improve their economies only by austerity measures falling hardest in the short run on the supporters who brought them to power. Whether they can survive and progress depends on the amount of "policy space" they can muster with donor support and their own political skills.
- With their depressed economies, the states of sub-Saharan Africa must have external financial support to carry out policy reform. However, in relieving economic distress such aid often weakens the incentives to make the hard policy choices essential to economic recovery and sustained long-term growth. Donors intent on supporting both a transition to democratic government and economic policy reform will face

the dilemma of whether to give priority to the political survival of the fledgling government or to economic change. In aid programs political and economic objectives have often been, and will often be, in conflict.[21]

These findings from the study of the politics of economic reform in Africa are remarkably parallel to some of the findings from the case studies of South Korea, the Philippines, Pakistan, and Mexico. For example, they highlight the dilemma of the linkage between economic and political reform. Although we can acknowledge that generous U.S. aid to the Aquino regime eroded the incentives for economic reform, that experience appears to have been another demonstration of the weakness of new democratic regimes in dealing with serious economic problems. Some of the other findings in the African study support the path being followed in Mexico of trying to realize substantial gains from trade liberalization and other economic reform measures before embarking on full-scale political liberalization. Overall, these findings suggest that a Third World state should probably become committed to a program of economic reform and a free market if it wishes to establish the basis for sustained development and eventually to realize the benefits of Western-style political pluralism.

There is no question that the case studies of Korea, the Philippines, Pakistan, and Mexico show some putative long-term successes for U.S. economic and noneconomic goals. In the case of the economic goals, the Korea study did not attempt to seriously assess the causal relationship. How important was U.S. economic aid in laying the foundation for the Korean economic miracle? The case study demonstrates that U.S. assistance gave Korea the opportunity to recover from the war and train its people and thus provided a base on which the Koreans themselves could shape their own economic future. The economic and military security the United States provided through the 1950s was the crucial foundation. In the other case studies the success of the economic development programs is much more problematic. Mexico appears to be about to embark on self-sustaining growth, but the Philippines and Pakistan continue to experience erratic growth and political instability while postponing badly needed economic reforms.

In assessing the movement toward noneconomic goals, some security goals were easily available for assessment. The political goal of democratization is more difficult, more long range, more complex in its cause-and-effect connections. In Korea, the United States has consistently encouraged free elections. In the early postwar years, Korean elections were "a sham," but more recently they have "evolved into very real events."[22] Similarly, in Pakistan knowledge of the strong U.S. attitude toward democracy contributed to a limited process of democratization in various periods. And in the Philippines the advent of Aquino's "people power" could be said to reflect U.S. stress on democratic values.

Such progress as there has been toward political stability and democracy in all four case studies suggests that economic development may indeed be necessary for the achievement of political maturity and stable democratic regimes. If so, however, the process has only commenced; durable political stability with democracy may be long in coming in each of these countries.

But even here the question of causality is difficult. Did U.S. aid, firmly attached to the word "democratization," actually sway the recipient rulers in the direction of political reform, or did it contribute to other kinds of success for the regime that helped it to endure and resist reform? If prosperity produced social elements that in turn produced turmoil that moved toward democratization, is this really the path Washington policymakers charted at the beginning? Can an unintended consequence be, in the end, an arrival at the same point as the intended goal, but still require the "unintended" classification because of the route taken? This is not idle theorizing: it goes to the heart of the extent of genuine success U.S. aid enjoyed in the Korean case and its meaning for future planning. But the fact remains that Korea appears able to defend itself and sustain an acceptable level of living without U.S. support. This was the prime goal of the U.S. program. The country also appears on its way to democracy, but political stability under democracy has not yet been adequately tested. In the other cases the record is still active, the outcome uncertain.

Paul Mosley also tried another approach to examining the effectiveness of U.S. aid, focusing on its goal of generating

enhanced goodwill for the United States among the recipient
countries. For the decade 1970 to 1980 Mosley examined the
UN voting record of the six major recipients of U.S. aid and the
six major recipients of Soviet aid. He further divided both
groups into those countries for which aid was rising and those
for which it was declining. Despite the doubtful ability of the
sole factor of UN voting records to carry the weight of such
generalization about the relationships, still no interesting
patterns appeared. Mosley concludes that "countries which use
aid as a means of buying political support get very little for
their money."[23] According to State Department sources, the
record of the last decade (1981–1990) has been similar and
relatively constant.[24] The voting record during the 1980s of the
three case-study countries that are UN members supports
Mosley's findings for the 1970s: on the basis of behavior in the
UN, the United States gets little for its money. The fact appears
to be that the three case-study countries appeared in most
cases to be voting on the merits of the issues as each saw
them. The principal conclusion must be that this superficial
test of aid effectiveness is likely to mislead.

More than attempting a scorecard of the success or failure,
the case studies and the overall study's conclusions seek reasons, relationships, and conditions that influence the results of
assistance, differential effects of different kinds of assistance,
the factors that can produce, not pride or disappointment, but
strategic shrewdness in future cases. Simple success or failure
is generally ambiguous, especially in the cases of increasing
availability of aid funds from other donors. Other donors have
been less inclined than the United States to attach political or
foreign policy conditions to their aid; the quid pro quo most
frequently required has been that aid funds be spent on goods
and services from the donor country. The fact that the United
States no longer had a monopoly of aid tended to make the
recipient more cavalier in his attitude toward meeting U.S.
conditions that were perceived as burdensome. On the other
hand, where the urgency of the U.S. national security objective
was marked, as in Pakistan and the Philippines, that fact, while
making the United States a more malleable donor, also permit-
ted the host to be more demanding of other donors.

Chapter III
Policy Guidelines

The Environment

U.S. aid programs have come under attack from many quarters and on many counts, but it is not only in U.S. programs that revisions are seen as necessary. The 1991 World Bank development report criticized development philosophies and tactics followed since the 1950s and recommended drastic changes for itself and other aid donors.[1] Other international organizations are also recommending startling new practices. European and Japanese aid officials have looked more closely at the performance of the developing countries, seeking ways to improve the record. All of these critics are concerned solely with the use of economic aid to advance economic growth and standards of living in the developing countries, although Europe and Japan are increasingly talking about relating aid to the human rights record of the recipient.[2] In short, new ideas about foreign aid are bubbling to the surface, ideas that are certain to stimulate discourse and more innovation.

In the United States, the U.S. Agency for International Development itself has added its voice to those of its critics. In May 1991, on the occasion of its thirtieth anniversary, USAID reported on a year-long agency review undertaken to enhance the effectiveness of the U.S. aid program in the dramatically altered foreign policy environment of the 1990s.[3] USAID's action plan was exclusively concerned with improved management practices to provide more flexibility and speed in its reactions to changed circumstances. USAID's self-criticism was limited to attempting to cope more effectively with the assignments the Congress has given it. It did not complain about conflicting goals, although it would have been justified in so doing. It did not ask to be relieved of any tasks, but it did indicate an awareness of having to assume some new ones, such as the environment.[4]

Pew Charitable Trusts, the sponsor of this study, has also supported an examination of the management of U.S. foreign aid. Unlike the CSIS study, the Pew study is principally concerned with the development and management of the U.S. program, through the attempt to create an integrated model of the program. Due for publication by Praeger Publishing of New York, it will carry the title *Modernizing Foreign Assistance: Resource Management as an Instrument of Foreign Policy.*

The timing for both Pew studies, its own on the management of the program and that of CSIS on the use of the program for noneconomic objectives, is appropriate to the moment. The administration has called for a complete overhaul of the program and new legislation rather than further revisions to the 1961 act.[5] The Overseas Development Council (ODC) has similarly recommended a total revamping (although with a different emphasis).[6] Concerned citizens, too, have recognized that the seismic changes in the world scene occurring since 1989 demand a reevaluation of all U.S. government programs related to international affairs.[7]

Once again, Penelope Hartland-Thunberg sets the scene for us in her assessment that the onslaught of criticisms and recommended changes appears to stem from the confluence of three independent developments: the dramatic change in the world scene; a swing in the social consensus concerning the proper role of government in society that has led to yet another shift in the accepted wisdom; and the sheer accumulation of experience with different patterns of economic development.

The end of the cold war, of course, offers the possibility of a sizable shift of resources away from defense to other favored uses at home and abroad. Most critics of the U.S. program, however (being sensitive to alternative competing demands for resources), do not recommend a larger foreign aid expenditure, but rather a reoriented one. Several critics—in the Congress, in ODC, and in our case studies, Ambassador Preeg especially—recommend a major shift in the U.S. program toward project aid, retaining the requirement that U.S. aid funds for this purpose be spent on U.S. goods and services, at least until U.S. competitors in world markets end their practice of tying their aid to their own exports.

The pendulum in human affairs, which after World War II swung to produce consensus in the West (stronger in some countries than in others) on the proper role of government in society, reversed its direction in the 1980s. Starting in the late 1940s the belief spread, first in the industrialized world, then through the developing world, that governments could and should solve such social problems as poverty, unemployment, health, education, old age, and housing. As social service programs expanded, so did the role of the government in the economy.

In the developing world, economic growth models typically assumed that lack of capital was the main factor inhibiting growth and that with adequate amounts of capital a developing country could enter a self-sustaining growth path by replacing imports with domestic production. A protective tariff wall and subsidies were acceptable government encouragement, at least temporarily.[8]

Emphasis in development programs continued to evolve, reflecting the new findings of research and practical experience. In the early 1970s a series of studies showed that in the developing world the poor were getting a smaller share of total output and also becoming absolutely poorer.[9] Such studies moved World Bank president Robert McNamara to shift the Bank's lending emphasis in order to benefit the rural poor. Country growth records showed great variation, especially after the oil price shocks of the 1970s and the debt crisis of the 1980s. The economic miracles in the four Asian tigers, which succeeded in maintaining the highest growth rates in the world without going into debt during the 1970s and 1980s, attracted attention throughout the developing world. The four tigers boasted of their commitment to export expansion and private enterprise.

Meanwhile in the industrialized West disillusionment with the role of government in the economy mounted. Europessimism, inflation, and then the worst recession in the postwar period helped to create doubts that the government *could* solve all social problems. The success of the United States in maintaining prosperity and expanding employment during the Reagan administration of the 1980s (in contrast to the record of most other industrialized countries) and the emergence of Japan as the world economic strongman helped to convince the world that the government was the main problem and that free and open markets were the solution.[10] The collapse of communism in the East provided the coup de grace to a belief in central planning and government ownership of industry. The pendulum had shifted; a new social consensus emerged emphasizing free markets, private enterprise, and democracy.

Whether *the* secret of sustained economic development has finally been found remains to be seen. A review of history leads to a certain skepticism over the durability of a social consensus. Nonetheless North and South, East and West today agree that the path to economic development moves through export expansion and free private enterprise and that eventually it will lead to democracy.

The 1991 World Bank development report reflected the new consensus. It urged Third World governments and aid donors to invest in people and liberalize markets. Stressing recent research findings, the Bank pointed to the development of human resources as of prime importance together with "effective government as a scarce resource to be employed sparingly and only where most needed."[11] It argued that provision of an adequate infrastructure is an appropriate and important government function. It noted that historically those developing countries that invested heavily in education and removed government-backed economic distortions grew at an average annual rate of 5.5 percent from 1965 to 1987, while those adopting only one of these policies grew at only 4 percent, and those adopting neither at only 3 percent annually. It observed that a country following the Bank's development strategies could in 20 years have twice the income of one that ignored them.

The report is refreshing in the courageous frankness with which it criticizes government corruption, inefficiency, and waste. If a country does not have a competent, efficient government, foreign aid is wasted; such a government should be a condition for external support.

The report's findings and recommendations were extended in a policy paper issued by the World Bank at the time of its 1991 annual meetings (with the IMF) in Bangkok.[12] There, and in the address by the Bank's new president (Lewis Preston) to the gathering of world bankers and finance people, alleviation of poverty was stated as the Bank's "overarching objective."

Thus developing countries must pursue growth policies that use their most plentiful resource, labor, and at the same time they must work to make labor more productive by investing in education, health, and family planning. In short, the World Bank has laid out a carefully conceived, integrated development strategy that unites old and new policies in an approach that, if followed, is potentially revolutionary.

Recent empirical research on developing countries by academics has supported and extended that of the Bank. Findings indicate that 80 percent of the variation in per capita income in these countries can be explained by population growth, saving, and education. Saving and education were found to be about equal: a 1 percent increase in the proportion of output devoted to education (or saving) leads to a sustained increase of about 1 percent (after a certain time lag) in the level of output per worker—that is, in productivity.[13] Rising productivity is essential for self-sustaining growth. More educated workers are able to use more sophisticated production techniques and thus require more physical capital, which implies more savings. High population increase, however, inhibits growth because it requires ever more savings to provide the human and physical capital investment necessary for increased productivity.

Both the World Bank and the IMF began to reflect the new consensus in their 1991 policy announcements. Both announced that military spending by developing countries would be considered in determining the level of their economic support programs in the Third World.[14] The fact that a number of developing countries had been spending more on arms than on health and education was noted. The United Nations Development Program (UNDP) made the same point in its 1991 Human Development Report, stressing that Third World countries should direct more of their expenditures toward "human priority" fields like health, education, and family planning.[15]

The UNDP has constructed a "Human Development Index," which it recommends as a basis for granting economic aid. Its index reflects life expectancy, adult literacy, and basic purchasing power for a "decent" living standard. It has also developed a "human freedom" index that seeks to relate freedom and development.[16]

The Bush administration's recommended changes in the U.S. foreign aid program concentrated on reducing the restrictions on aid disbursements that had accumulated since 1961 in a series of amendments initiated by the Congress. The administration had been complaining for several years of its inability to use foreign aid as a tool of foreign policy because flexibility had disappeared from the prevailing legislation.

The argument with the Congress is largely political, but what is of interest is that both the president and the Congress continue to view aid disbursements as an instrument of foreign policy. Both parties agree that aid should be used to reward good behavior and punish bad (e.g., in regard to human rights, nuclear proliferation); the argument is over where the decision should be made. Despite the excitement over new growth philosophies, no voice on either end of Pennsylvania Avenue is heard to recommend that economic aid should be used to foster economic development. Such calls are confined to organizations like the ODC and members of academia.

Commentary on the Guidelines and Recommendations

The general guidelines that emerge from the analyses of this study, plus a description of that analysis itself, appear earlier in this report. The exceedingly rich case studies have some clear areas of mutual consistency in the relationship of the strategy and instruments of economic assistance to the pursuit of the noneconomic policy objectives of the United States and some of its allies, especially national security, democratization, and internal stability.

The end of the cold war and the removal of superpower rivalry allows us to see more clearly the challenges that contain dangers and opportunities that are no less poignant than the U.S.-Soviet confrontation used to be. They include poverty and disease, the narcotics trade, ethnic strife and the abuse of human rights, mass migration to escape oppressive conditions, the proliferation of nuclear, chemical, and biological arms and the means to send them over great distances, maldistribution of natural resources, and environmental degradation. History may show that any one of these should have been recognized as more lethal than the Soviet menace. History will be impressed by what got us, not what might have got us.

An interesting characteristic of this gallery of post-cold war threats is that foreign economic assistance has been discussed in relation to ameliorating each of them, although, in some cases, in the form of crude bribery. Even in the latter type of situation, the bribe intended to cause a country to adopt certain policies relative to its arsenal or its rain forest should be informed by the findings of this study if the odds of success are to be maximized. The distinctions made between the immediate and the distant, and between the short term and the long term, in defining objectives, the lesson of the frozen spigot and the calculations it must inspire about what increases or reduces leverage, and the relationship among multiple objectives for the same program all come into play.

The vocabulary should not interfere with clear thought about the situation. Americans have grown used to using "security" when they mean "military." So, as new menaces to their well-being emerged, the rhetorical flourish of calling these menaces "security" threats became common practice. It has become a vehicle of hyperbole. "Security," in this new context, really means "high politics," the topics and situations about which leaders talk at the summit, for which governments fall, and which might lead to either military action or dangerous chaos.

If this new agenda is approached in its broadest form— with general goals and a very long time frame—then its relation to economic assistance is less problematical but measurement of success will be next to impossible. The thesis would be that, in the long run, the best way, possibly the only way, to solve the problems of narcotics, mass migration, abuse of human rights, nuclear proliferation, and environmental degradation in the Third World is to improve the economies of these countries so that the governments and the people will gain the physical means and the political will to cope with these demands. (This is the point made repeatedly at the 1992 Rio environmental summit by representatives of Third World nations.) Therefore, according to this theory, most U.S. economic aid should be directed at improving economic performance over the longer term rather than at short-term solutions based on gaining political influence over the governments in power. At a time of expanding budgets and low international political tension, this comforting (and probably mostly correct) thesis would be the suitable foundation for a large part of the U.S. foreign assistance program. *But under the current circumstances, it would be extremely vulnerable politically and the findings of the current study indicate that the challenge to it would have some legitimate grounds in terms of past experience.*

This is especially the case if what is being asked of the recipient is politically difficult reform and policy change. It is perhaps the Korean case that best dramatizes the fact, a thoroughly expectable phenomenon, that aid is effective in obtaining performance and policies toward which the recipient leadership was already disposed, and that, on the contrary, only the most perfectly tight and credible connection between the aid spigot, clear objectives, and donor singleness of purpose can hope to produce results in the face of serious reluctance on the part of the recipient. When the objective is very general, very long-term, and likely to stretch beyond the scope and time of the aid, *the odds of success are at their lowest and the present analysis gives little ground for optimism. Conversely, the best odds obtain when the objective is economic, has great proximity to (or is exactly the same as) the specific work to be carried out by the aid project, is short-term, is genuinely supported by the political leadership of the receiving country (including important competing factions), is not burdened with secondary objectives, and is distributed, delayed, or suspended according to a credible and tight connection to the donor's insistence on clear performance standards, whether the donor is the United States alone, the United States and allies, or an international agency.*

"Immediate" often takes the form of short term as opposed to long term, but the two factors are not necessarily the same.[17] In the example of the dam constructed with foreign economic assistance, prosperity in the region, a goal of the project (but not the most immediate goal, which was the building of the dam, or even the subsequent goal, which was

the distribution of energy to the region), may come very
slowly, but as a direct result of the dam and the plentiful and
inexpensive power it generated. Or prosperity might come
quickly if, in the course of the construction, they strike oil. In
this case the aid planners can take no real credit for the quick
prosperity. They have just produced an unintended consequence of the nicest sort. The point is that the study's findings,
and the informal confirmation rendered by the regional study
programs of CSIS, relate far more strongly to the question of
directness, of the immediate consequences, than to the simple
question of time.

The prospective utility of various means of allied cooperation in extending economic assistance to achieve the objectives
of the new agenda does not appear to escape the implications
of the findings *except* that (1) *the effort to make a statement of
political support for hard choices by the recipient regime will,
in most cases, be aided, and the statement amplified, by
having a phalanx of donor countries, rather than just one,
behind it* and (2), working in the other direction, *the leverage
provided by the credible ability and willingness to control the
aid spigot according to recipient country performance is
necessarily weakened by the undoubtedly legitimate pre-
sumption that a group of countries will find it harder to agree
on and coordinate reductions and suspensions in the aid
flow.* The last point refers, of course, to situations in which
several countries, either in a consortium or independently,
give economic assistance to the same recipient for the same
general objectives. This maximizes the difficulty of agreement
on issues of controlling the aid flow, and also maximizes the
ability of the receiving country to play one donor off against
the other, a practice at which some Third World regimes
became adept during the cold war. If the donors are simply
contributors to an international agency, such as the IMF, with
a powerful reputation for relating recipient performance to aid
flow, then this drawback to allied cooperation is eliminated.

A crucial factor in the above formulations about the maxi-
mizing of chances for success is one to which U.S. policymakers have occasionally been surprisingly oblivious during
the postwar period: the relation to perceived recipient inter-

ests. All four cases contain this element, although it is less noteworthy in the Mexican case—and therein lies a lesson. It is consistently true that where the interests of the recipient country and the noneconomic goals of the United States coincided, such use of U.S. economic aid accomplished its purpose. Both the donor and recipient benefited. When, however, the U.S. goals conflicted with the interests of the recipient country, the aid failed. But this initial point, made earlier, needs modification in light of the cases. In the first place, the success or failure turns on the question of the interests of the receiving country *as perceived by its ruling group.* Even finer, the pivotal question is not so much the interest of the receiving country in the eyes of the ruling group as it is *the interests of the ruling group itself, as it perceives them.* Even this needs refinement in light of the evidence, for the people and factions who may be powerful enough to be rightly considered a part of the ruling group may not be in agreement among themselves. *The aid, if seen as playing a role in their internal struggle, will then have one or more powerful antagonistic counter-constituencies.* Some of these, or the ruling group as a whole, may see the aid's objectives as actually threatening. Worse yet, this perception may not be present at the beginning, when the aid is negotiated, but only subsequently. This can come about through a change in the ruling group itself, or a change in their perceptions. If, for example, autocrats and oligarchs are currently watching events in Thailand and elsewhere in the Far East, they may conclude that the evidence of these new difficulties means that enormous national economic success will not assure a tranquil period of rule *if* it creates a modernizing middle class that is bound to become dissatisfied with what it considers to be a form of rule inappropriate for the country's new status and character. Certain kinds and levels of economic development will then be seen as a threat, and the aid as its vehicle.

A particular temptation of the new agenda will be that of making single aid programs serve multiple goals. The study indicates the unlikelihood of clear predictable success in hitting targets other than the principal one. In fact, what they show is worse than that. *Not only must one be pessimistic*

about the achieving of secondary and tertiary goals in eco-
nomic assistance, but it is probable that the effort to do so
will jeopardize the achievement of the primary (overt) goal.

Where the aid is intended to produce leverage for reform or
a certain recipient-country policy line, success is difficult
enough without diffusing the pressure. It is even possible to
multiply the difficulty by mixing in some of our guideline
elements. If the recipient country believes that the spigot is
frozen because of Washington's preoccupation with Goal A, or
even that while it may not be frozen, but will move according
to the performance relative to Goal A, it can be expected to
pay little heed to Washington's other goals.

So the appeal of the new focus of the economic aid program could be negated if the new program is saddled with
additional goals only obliquely related to its most immediate
objectives.

Part of the tension here is between domestic politics and
overseas reality. *Loading a program with multiple goals may*
both diminish its chances for accomplishment and also
increase its chances for promotion by the administration and
approval by the Congress. Removing these multiple goals from
the economic aid program to other parts of the government's
budget, where they are still relevant, would simplify compre-
hension and enhance the effectiveness of economic aid. But
U.S. constituency politics may make it difficult to take advan-
tage of this clear lesson of the analysis of cold war economic
assistance (of all kinds).

In fact, most of the participants in the study, scholars,
specialists, and officials, predicted tough sledding for appropriations that have as their principal objective the sustained
growth of (even selected) foreign economies. The key to
making this attractive to the American people has not yet been
found. The cold war is no longer available for that purpose.
The kind of appeal made to some publics in Western Europe,
which drew on the colonial heritage to impose (often successfully) a feeling of responsibility for the well-being of certain
Third World countries, usually former colonies, is not available
to Washington and shows signs of getting threadbare in some
European capitals. An examination of Japan would be interest-

ing on this score. Is the key to political viability of this kind of development assistance, in U.S. politics, to translate these objectives into markets and profitable overseas economic activity benefiting the United States? CSIS's Edward Luttwak is currently at work on the development of a set of strategic *geoeconomic* theories; for example, he is examining the success of the Japanese government in making overseas development assistance relatively uncontroversial in Japan. Some of it, of course, is tied to the development of markets for Japan. But even the purely altruistic easily cleared domestic political hurdles with the argument that it was necessary to pacify a world that might be bothered by the hard edge of Japanese selfish aggressiveness. Luttwak says that moral issues, the idea that Japan has a responsibility, is beginning to creep into the debate in Japan. If it does, Luttwak predicts that aid and other Japanese overseas practices will become more controversial in Japanese domestic politics.

One phenomenon that the case studies and the CSIS regional studies programs appear to demonstrate would be striking and important if it could fairly be labeled a finding. Rigorous scholarship demands, however, that it be left as a hint rather than a finding; the evidence—the number of in-depth case studies and questions examined in the case studies themselves—is insufficient for more than a suggestive pattern. The pattern is this: *large aid recipients, such as the Philippines and Pakistan, have poor economic growth and development records, whereas in recent years Mexico, not a recipient of official economic assistance, has been doing remarkably well.* The problem here is not that Mexico, a nonrecipient of the type of aid that is the predominant focus of this study, was included; the problem is that there are not other cases with its profile to permit a better-substantiated general finding.

Most of the new agenda of foreign policy objectives is long-term and ongoing. Problems of population, poverty, environmental protection, narcotics, and the like are not fixed for all time overnight. They are long-term problems requiring generations to solve. And even after the developing country achieves the capacity itself to sustain the effort without foreign aid, constant vigilance will be required.

The experience of economic assistance examined in this study leads to the suggestion that relating these goals to possible economic assistance programs should involve the recognition that there will be *stages* to the effort. Drawing on the cases examined and others, one can postulate, for most items on the future agenda:

Stage One: Announcement and initial delivery of the aid as a statement of political support for hard choices the recipient regime is being asked to make. This study, and common usage, too often speak of the political difficulty of such actions as environmental protection. That is, of course, too simple. Such actions may have a very large and strong constituency in the recipient country. Part of the strategic planning of both donor and recipient should then be the challenge of mobilizing that support. But even in a case where a million citizens of a region want relief from foul air and fetid water, a few powerful industrialists may still be capable of making pollution reduction very difficult politically for the regime. The point here is not to assume that all the political weight in such instances is with the internal opposition.

Stage Two: Maintenance of pressure in the direction of the policies and action sought through a credible carrot-and-stick furnished by real control over the spigot of aid. Essential though this leverage may be, it is difficult and, as the cases show, problem-filled. To the extent that the pressure is broadly visible, it will be labeled by opponents as interference with the sovereignty of the recipient state. And if the aid is related to serious long-term projects, any idea that the flow of aid will be arbitrary and mercurial will erode the confidence of people whose commitment and investment may be necessary for the project. The latter paradox is overcome to the extent that the flow is openly related to the *efficiency of resource use* and, therefore, to the same presumed objectives of those necessary participants.

And, in fact, this rubric of efficient resource use can subsume many of the possible goals. A regime that intimidates its citizens with human rights abuses will injure their productivity and enterprise. A country trapped in static poverty because its population grows more rapidly than its output will lack resources to provide the basics of education and health required for higher productivity. Such a country will also generate flows of economic migrants that may destabilize its neighbors. Narcotics production and trade are a source of income but must be replaced if the trade is to be eliminated. Corruption in high places is clearly a waste of resources and is likely to be accompanied by excessive militarization to keep the regime in power. But the case studies show that this theme is no panacea. A judgment of efficiency about resource use requires accord on the best use of those resources, which is a political, not economic, question. The record of difficulties traced in the cases is a record of different parties having different priority objectives.

Despite the advantages of doing so in many situations, a policy of directing most economic aid through international institutions does not appear to be politically feasible in the near future. There would be little or no support for such a move in the United States or from most other major bilateral donors because the source of its benefit becomes difficult to pinpoint. If all aid funds were pooled and contracts awarded on the merits of price and quality *without* subsidies, the benefit to the donors would be in the more productive use of their resources, a benefit that is often politically insufficient for the donors.

Some poor and backward societies have accomplished economic miracles as aid recipients. Although foreign aid's aggregate contribution to the Korean or Taiwanese economic miracle may have been quantitatively minor, it appears to have been crucial. By no means can foreign aid be dismissed as useless for purposes of economic development. Moreover, as a foreign policy tool, foreign aid is popular in official Washington. The administration finds it useful to have resources available to add to its perceived leverage for specific foreign policy initiatives. The Congress finds it useful as a means of expressing its approval for or dismay at the policies of other countries. Foreign aid is viewed as one additional instrument in the box of policy tools available to U.S. officials. Perhaps it often does not work very well, but it is seen to be better than nothing. Despite this popularity in Washington, one must anticipate (1) a much tighter pinch on available resources, meaning (2) a closer look at proposed programs, and (3), for at least the most serious administration officials and congressional members and staffers, a desire to use this historic juncture to learn from analysis in the hope of choosing sounder objectives and increasing the odds of their achievement.

And many of the *new* foreign policy/national security objectives of the United States are shared by some or all other donors as well as by most of the recipient countries. Europe, for example, is acutely concerned over potential waves of migration from Eastern Europe, the former Soviet Union, and elsewhere and has already recognized that aid for economic development in the homelands of the potential migrants is an expenditure in its own interest. Japan is, if anything, even more immigrant-averse than Europe; much of its aid to China and other parts of the area is to forestall any attempts to migrate to Japan. The intensity of all donors' concern over environmental degradation, nuclear proliferation, narcotics, and human rights has mounted in recent years. On these matters more collaboration among the donors through support of the multilateral agencies' programs of conditionality will be increasingly appealing.

Albeit inadvertently, the United States has already made a start on the use of foreign aid for the new foreign policy objectives. As the Mexican case study makes clear, the extension of the Canadian Free Trade Agreement to Mexico by means of NAFTA is aimed at a long-term correction of both the narcotics and migration problems that Mexico presents for the United States. In this case the stimulus to Mexican economic growth is sought through trade expansion because Mexico refuses more traditional forms of economic aid. Despite the concerns of some environmentalists that the treaty permits the export of pollution by U.S. industry, most analysts believe that measures taken to protect the environment increase with income.

The United States should take the lead in organizing support for all of these policy objectives among all aid donors, urging each to make its own aid conditional upon appropriate behavior by the recipient and, where appropriate, to direct aid funds through multilateral organizations that support and practice such conditionality.

Analysis of U.S. aid machinery, when combined with this study's findings about the relationship between aid objectives and the conditions for success and failure, may lead to the conclusion that, to support the new foreign policy objectives, the United States needs new legislation. The current analysis, by itself, does not carry that far. Some of those who participated in the study came to the conclusion that the 1961 Foreign Assistance legislation should be retired and that the new mandate should reflect in the objectives of the act U.S. concerns about human needs (poverty, health, education), human rights, destabilizing migration flows, environmental quality, nuclear proliferation, and narcotics control. But these personal views required the addition of other information and insights to the current analysis.

One potential aid use deserves special comment. Recent research underlying the importance of education in economic growth is in harmony with the intuitive judgment of many participants. It makes sense that a person who can read and write will be more productive than one who cannot. U.S. bilateral aid programs could supplement the human resource development efforts of the World Bank by stressing, in the allocation of its aid funds, aid to education in the poorest countries and in the urban slums of the middle-income countries. It is a form of specialization that would seem to reflect U.S. values and current U.S. emphasis at home. Indeed, education as a priority area for aid has a rich literature. But the problem is that education is a management-intensive sector for aid, so it is not where most of the money is likely to go.

The United States in the past has largely withdrawn from the international competition for large infrastructure projects in the developing world because most of its aid resources have been used for cash payments to favored developing countries for security/foreign policy support. The end of the cold war will release resources formerly used for this purpose. Infrastructure projects are commercially rewarding because they entail not only large-scale purchases of engineering services and capital equipment, but a future flow of parts and other orders to equipment suppliers. Infrastructure projects have a larger impact on trade flows than any other form of aid. Infrastructure financing plays a central role for the World Bank and other bilateral programs. In opting out of this competition in the past the United States has sacrificed its own economic interests in favor of other foreign policy concerns.

The authors of the case studies make some of these recommendations and often cite the advantages of directing aid through multilateral agencies. None goes so far as to state as an ideal that all or most development aid should be directed to multilateral agencies.[18] Nor does any case study author recommend that U.S. bilateral aid specialize in education. They all recommend that economic aid be used for purposes of economic development,[19] although the Mexican paper is concerned that the relation between economic reform and political stability has not been clearly analyzed.[20] The Korean paper urges that donors recognize the possibility that economic aid, if successful, will eventually create new competitors on the world scene.[21] Both the Philippine paper and the Korean urge that aid be targeted especially toward specific, developmentally sound projects;[22] aid to education and infrastructure projects fits this condition. The Philippine paper makes a strong case for placing economic aid for military objectives in the defense budget.[23]

Similarly, the Philippine study foreshadows the new emphasis of the World Bank by recommending that aid be conditioned on recipient performance and give more emphasis to health, education, and small-scale agriculture.[24] Finally, Ambassador Preeg stresses the need to reevaluate and update the entire U.S. foreign aid program to recognize changes on the world scene. He also recommends that the United States integrate aid, trade, and investment policies to promote growth in the Third World and to strengthen U.S. export competitiveness.[25] In general, the guidelines and recommendations in this and the initial section carry those in the country studies to their aggregate logical conclusion, some of them foreshadowed in the Mexican case.

But the force of the findings is *not* to replace the superfluity of old aid-program goals with a new list. Instead, they specify the conditions to be met for a program to be free of the charge that it does not take account of the lessons of U.S.

postwar aid experience. They suggest the need for credible leverage to back up the demands made on the recipient country and the fairly narrow range of reasonable objectives available to any single aid or other resource-transfer program. Obviously, some flexibility should be provided to the president in administering the program; the Congress, however, should ensure that the flexibility provision is not abused, including the abuse of ignoring previous experience.

In any event, the "new" post-cold war agenda, that range of challenges described in this report, is not likely to be manifested as legislated *goals* of action programs in future initiatives, but as *constraints and conditions* applied to condition the behavior of elements within the host country. *This is an important distinction because it facilitates the replication of such conditions and constraints in the aid programs of other like-minded donors,* even in cases where the goals and means of the projects are otherwise quite different from those of the United States.

The universality of support for the new U.S. foreign policy goals is unique in its growing strength; these matters are important to individuals around the world, affecting daily lives in a way that the cold war never did. As a consequence the new goals are better able to unite peoples as well as governments in developed and developing countries, a fact likely to facilitate significant international collaboration in pursuit of the goals.

A final note falls outside the findings of the analysis. Although the study provides crucial guidance on how to succeed or fail in the pursuit of noneconomic objectives with the use of various forms of economic assistance, and although the strength of the consensus that may surround some of the goals of the "new security agenda" will certainly lead Washington and other capitals (often at the urging of the potential recipients) to try to achieve goals in these realms using the economic assistance tool, a prevailing view among the scholars who worked on this study, not proved by the findings but certainly informed by the experience of arriving at them, is that economic aid should be used primarily to help improve the performance of the economies of the Third World in accordance with free-market principles and practices. Success will produce, country by country, a range of unintended consequences—turmoil here and stability there, radical politics here and moderate politics there, cooperation here and competition there, ethnic-peace-through-prosperity here and ethnic-conflict-over-the-spoils there. But the unprovable, incalculable judgement of most of these scholars is that aid used in this way will produce, even for the U.S. taxpayer, more that is benign than malign.

Notes

Part One. Conclusions and Recommendations

Starting at the End

1. This report's use of "goals," "priorities," and "means" is explained in a long footnote at the beginning of Part II, Analysis.

The Guidelines

1. Michael J. Mazarr, "Investing in Security: U.S. Economic Assistance and Noneconomic Goals in Korea" (CSIS, Washington, D.C., April 1991) (hereafter *Korea*).

M. Delal Baer, "U.S. Economic Policy and the Unconventional Security Agenda in Mexico" (CSIS, Washington, D.C., March 1991) (hereafter *Mexico*).

Shireen T. Hunter, "Investing in Security: The Case of Pakistan" (CSIS, Washington, D.C., May 1991) (hereafter *Pakistan*).

Ernest H. Preeg, *Neither Fish nor Fowl: U.S. Economic Aid to the Philippines for Noneconomic Objectives,* CSIS Significant Issues Series, vol. 13, no. 3 (Washington, D.C.: CSIS, 1991) (hereafter *Philippines*).

Full texts of all reports, including the African study, are available from the CSIS Publications Office.

2. Center for Strategic and International Studies, *The Politics of Economic Reform in Sub-Saharan Africa,* Final report of a study sponsored by the U.S. Agency for International Development (Washington, D.C.: CSIS, March 1992) (hereafter *Africa*).

3. *Africa,* ix.

4. *Korea,* 15, 31; *Philippines,* 10.

5. *Korea,* 104.

The Case Findings

1. In general, the case studies view economic aid as a transfer of resources on concessional terms between two sovereign states. Starting from this broad definition, however, each study adjusts its use depending on the specific content and the availability of information. Data on Official Develop-

ment Assistance (ODA) are much more readily available and more reliable, for example, than private-sector flows on concessional terms.

2. *Mexico,* 5.

Part Two. Analysis

1. From its beginning to this final report, this study has not adhered to certain word usages that would be consistent with the legislation and official communications about U.S. foreign assistance, but being thus consistent would have created confusion for nonadepts of the aid art unless laboriously explained with each use.

Strictly speaking, the only objectives for U.S. foreign economic assistance are those in the basic legislation. To speak of priorities among the explicit or implicit objectives of that legislation is to violate it. Beyond the base legislation, all things achieved or intended in individual country programs are not "objectives," they are "means." But, outside the chambers of Washington, putting a region's economy on its feet or giving it the means to defend itself from a rapacious neighbor are most certainly ends, objectives, to all those involved, not mere means. Realizing our transgression, therefore, it is useful in this work to recognize that objectives exist at a series of levels, that parties involved may have different objectives, and that priorities are to be distinguished, *must* be distinguished, to make observed (or intended) behavior coherent. But in each case, one could rightfully ask "*Whose* primary objective?"

This difference in usage is easy to gloss over for purposes of the current dialogue, but not necessarily so easy in future practice. For example, what complications will arise from the fact that stimulating the economic development of foreign countries is not a recognized goal in U.S. aid legislation?

Chapter I — The Primacy of the National Security Purpose of Aid

1. Penelope Hartland-Thunberg, *The Political and Strategic Importance of Exports,* CSIS Significant Issues Series, vol. I, no. 3 (Washington, D.C.: CSIS, 1979), 4–10.

2. David A. Baldwin in *Foreign Aid and American Foreign Policy* (New York: Praeger, 1966), 3, defines foreign aid as "a technique of statecraft. It is in other words a means by which one nation tries to get other nations to act in desired ways."

3. Public Law 87–195, September 4, 1961.

4. The Statement of Policy in chapter I of the act was amended almost every year, but not until the 1978 Act did this Statement include a reference to humanitarian objectives. The 1978 Act said, after restating the national security reasons for U.S. foreign aid, "Furthermore, the Congress reaffirms the traditional humanitarian ideals of the American people and renews its commitment to assist people in developing countries to eliminate hunger, poverty, illness and ignorance." Public Law 95–425, October 6, 1978.

5. *Vital Speeches of the Day,* vol. 14 (New York: City News Publishing Company, 1949), 332.

6. Chart 1 includes Marshall Plan aid in "other bilateral."

7. Paul Mosley, *Foreign Aid: Its Defense and Reform* (Lexington: University Press of Kentucky, 1987), 21.

8. The proposal had been discussed earlier that spring in a speech by Dean Acheson, the under secretary of state, who was substituting for Truman. See Foreword by Clark Clifford in Robert J. Donovan, *The Second Victory: The Marshall Plan and the Postwar Revival of Europe* (New York: Madison Books, 1988), 8.

9. R. Dennett and R. Turner, eds., *Documents on American Foreign Relations,* vol. 9, *1947* (Princeton, N.J.: Princeton University Press, 1949), 9.

10. Passage was accelerated by the Red Army invasion of Czechoslovakia in February 1948. Donovan, *Second Victory,* 48.

11. Ibid., 47.

12. *Vital Speeches of the Day,* vol. 15, no. 8 (February 1, 1949), 226–228. See also Stephen Browne, *Foreign Aid in Practice* (New York: New York University Press, 1990), 14–20.

13. Dennett and Turner, *Documents on American Foreign Relations,* vol. 9, *1947,* p. 647.

14. "An Act to Provide for Assistance to Greece and Turkey, Approved May 27, 1947," in Dennett and Turner, *Documents on American Foreign Relations,* vol. 9, *1947,* pp. 674–677.

15. Dennett and Turner, *Documents on American Foreign Relations,* vol. 11, *1949,* p. 626.

16. Ibid., vol. 13, *1951,* p. 1, citing the administrator of the Technical Assistance Program before the Senate Committee on Foreign Relations and Armed Services on August 6, 1951.

17. *Korea,* 73; Robert Packenham, *Liberal America and the Third World: Political Ideas in Foreign Aid and Social Science* (Princeton, N.J.: Princeton University Press, 1973), 315.

18. Mosley, *Foreign Aid,* 23.

19. *Midyear Economic Report of the President and the Council of Economic Advisers* (Washington, D.C., July 1951), 7. In the early years of its history the Council issued semiannual economic reports.

20. *Economic Report of the President and the Council of Economic Advisers* (Washington, D.C., January 1959), 59.

21. Ibid., 1958, p. 72; 1961, p. 58.

22. The President's Committee to Study the U.S. Military Assistance Program, *Final Report* (Washington, D.C., August 17, 1959), 146, 137.

23. Quoted in Mosley, *Foreign Aid,* 45.

24. Ibid., 25.

25. Ernest Graves, "Security Assistance and Arms Sales," *The Washington Quarterly* 14, no. 3 (Summer 1991): 50; *Korea,* 71–87; Commission on Security and Economic Assistance, *A Report to the Secretary of State* (Carlucci Commission) (Washington, D.C., November 1983), 26.

26. Richard E. Bissell, "After Foreign Aid—What?" *The Washington Quarterly* 14, no. 3 (Summer 1991): 23.

27. For example, the importance of social institutions to the process of economic development is being explored in the research of (among others) Douglass C. North, who collates the work of historians, political scientists, anthropologists, and economists in examining the role of institutions in the lack of economic growth. "Institutions," *Journal of Economic Perspectives* 5, no. 6 (Winter 1991): 97–112.

28. Carlucci Commission, 26.

29. Eliott Berg, "Recent Trends and Issues in Development Strategies and Development Assistance," in R. E. Feinberg and R. M. Avakov, *From Confrontation to Cooperation?* Overseas

Development Council, U.S. Third World Perspectives no. 15 (New Brunswick, N.J.: Transaction Publishers, 1991), 70.

30. John W. Sewell, "Foreign Aid for a New World Order," *The Washington Quarterly* 14, no. 3 (Summer 1991): 38; Carlucci Commission, 22.

31. See *Philippines*, 22–23, for a discussion of the difficulties of international comparisons of ODA levels.

32. *Korea*, 118.

33. *Pakistan*, 106d.

34. *Philippines*, 22.

35. *Mexico*, 9.

36. Mosley, *Foreign Aid*, 31.

37. Penelope Hartland-Thunberg bemoaned these trends as early as 1979 in *The Political and Strategic Importance of Exports*, CSIS Significant Issues Series, vol. I, no. 3 (Washington, D.C.: CSIS, 1979). For a theoretical discussion of aid motivations, see Bruno S. Frey, *International Political Economics* (Oxford and New York: Basil Blackwell, 1984), 86 ff.

Chapter II — Foreign Economic Aid as an Instrument of National Security Policy

1. *Korea*, 7.

2. *Pakistan*, 110–111.

3. *Philippines*, 7.

4. Ibid., 10.

5. *Mexico*, 26.

6. Ibid., 26–27.

7. Ibid., 17–18.

8. Ibid., 12.

9. *Korea*, 44–60.

10. Ibid., 90.

11. Ibid., 98–99.

12. Ibid., 19.

13. Ibid., 32.

14. *Philippines*, 1–3.

15. *Pakistan*, 84.

16. Ibid., 88.

17. Ibid., 116.

18. Ibid., 53.

19. Ibid., 90–91.

20. Ibid., 118.

21. *Africa,* viii–ix.

22. *Korea,* 28.

23. Mosley, *Foreign Aid,* 32–38, quotation on p. 38.

24. *Voting Practices in the United Nations,* an unsigned, undated report from the files of the State Department's Bureau for International Organization Affairs, covering selected years from the 1970s through 1988; *Report to Congress on Voting Practices in the United Nations, 1990.*

Chapter III — Policy Guidelines

1. World Bank, *World Development Report 1991: The Challenge of Development* (Oxford: Oxford University Press, 1991).

2. *Far Eastern Economic Review,* August 22, 1991, p. 14, and November 21, 1991, p. 80; Kaoru Okuizumi, "How Japan Can Fight for Human Rights," *Asian Wall Street Journal Weekly,* November 4, 1991, p. 16.

3. U.S. Agency for International Development, *Management Action Plan* (Washington, D.C., May 1991).

4. Ibid., 9.

5. *Washington Post,* May 9, 1991, p. A-19. In the Congress, the House of Representatives made essentially the same recommendations in June 1989 (H.R. 2655).

6. *Journal of Commerce,* May 17, 1991, p. 1.

7. *The Washington Quarterly* 14, no. 3 (Summer 1991): 23–56, featured a cluster of articles on "Foreign Assistance After the Cold War."

8. See Geoff M. Meier, ed., *Leading Issues in Economic Development,* 5th ed. (New York: Oxford University Press, 1989), 82–92, for a summary of analytical perspectives.

9. E.g., Irma Adelman and Cynthia Taft Morris, *Economic Growth and Social Equity in Developing Countries* (Stanford, Calif.: Stanford University Press, 1973); International Labor Organization, *Employment, Growth and Basic Needs: A One-World Problem* (Geneva: ILO, 1976).

10. Of the four tigers and Japan, only Hong Kong *practiced* free markets and private enterprise. In the others, the role of

the government was extensive, although they all claimed that they were practitioners of private enterprise and capitalism.

11. *Financial Times,* July 8, 1991, p. 10.

12. *Financial Times,* October 23, 1991, p. 4.

13. National Bureau of Economic Research, *NBER Digest,* March 1991, p. 2.

14. *Financial Times,* May 2, 1991, p. 6.

15. *Financial Times,* May 22, 1991, p. 4; *Journal of Commerce,* May 22, 1991, p. 3.

16. *Far Eastern Economic Review,* June 13, 1991, p. 20.

17. Attention is called to the discussion of terms in the long footnote at the beginning of Part Two, Analysis.

18. *Pakistan* recommends a larger share (p. 121).

19. *Korea,* 28; *Pakistan,* 120–121; *Philippines,* 28.

20. *Mexico,* 26.

21. *Korea,* 32.

22. *Korea,* 31; *Philippines,* 28.

23. *Philippines,* 27.

24. Ibid., 28.

25. Ibid.

CSIS BOOKS of Related Interest

The United States and the Pacific Islands
John C. Dorrance

Twenty-two Pacific island states and territories lie astride or are proximate to critical air and sea routes linking the United States with Asia and Australia, but they generally have been ignored by Washington. The author, whose knowledge of the South Pacific was unsurpassed, evaluates the policy environment, the evolution of U.S. interest and policies, and challenges for these and related issues. He concludes with a discussion of new low-cost regional strategies.

CSIS Washington Paper/Praeger   188 pp. $14.95 (pb) ____
                                                      $37.95 (hb) ____

Conflict Resolution and Democratization in Panama: Implications for U.S. Policy
Eva Loser, editor

The manner in which Panamanian dictator Manuel Noriega was removed from power has far-ranging implications for Panama's political and economic renewal and for the role of outside powers in that process. This volume examines the issues of conflict resolution both internally and bilaterally, post-invasion democratization efforts, and the lessons for U.S. policy in promoting democratic rule.

CSIS Significant Issues Series   95 pp. $9.95____

U.S. Foreign Policy after the Cold War
Brad Roberts, editor

Leading practitioners and analysts in the foreign policy field explore ways in which U.S. interests and policies abroad are changing with the passing of the cold war. Some chapters evaluate how long-standing policy priorities and instruments carry over into the new era. Others explore new challenges posed by the environment and a globalizing economy.

CSIS Copublished Book/MIT Press   367 pp. $14.95____

To order: Make checks payable to **CSISBOOKS.**
                 Add $3.50 for postage and handling.   **Total** ____

Send books to: _____

_____

_____

☐ Please send a Publications Catalogue

CSISBOOKS   1800 K Street, NW, Suite 400   Washington, D.C. 20006
Telephone (202) 775-3119 FAX (202) 775-3190